# 31 Days to *Lovely*:

## A Journey of Forgiveness

2$^{nd}$ Edition

Sarah Hawkes Valente

Cover art: "Lovely" by Cammie Jarvis

Cover Design by Danielle Designs: www.danielle-designs.com

Photos by Sarah Hawkes Valente

31 Days to Lovely: A Journey of Forgiveness
Foreword by Ellyn McCall
Edited by Beth Hawkes Fuellbier
KINGDOM TWINDOM PUBLICATIONS
A division of WHATEVER IS LOVELY PUBLICATIONS

Visit our website at www.kingdomtwindom.net

For Kevin
in loving memory


For Brian
because God brings forth beauty from ashes

For Ashley, Danielle, Ellyn, Cammie, Renee, Tiffani and
Emily –without whom this book would be a draft in a
drawer

For Beth, my loving cousin and merciless editor

For Mom, who watched my kids so that I could drink coffee
and write

For Dad, who has always wanted me to write a book

# Contents

# *Foreword:*

    Sarah Valente is one of my closest friends. Our friendship has been built over email and phone lines, through hours of shared laughter and tears, and because we have *entirely* too much in common. The advent of the Internet age has brought with it many things both positive and negative, but one of the best, to me, is the capacity to feel less alone. The Internet opens up our society so that we are never the only one going through any given situation. There is someone else out there who has been there, right there, wherever it is that we are.

    In the first email Sarah ever sent me, she wrote three sentences that would stick with me through a lot of trials. "I have been there. You can survive this. I have hope for you." She was someone safe, who understood, who I could go to when it felt like no one else could see where I was coming from, who I could trust to be both empathetic and call me out when I needed it. By the time we spoke on the phone for the first time, it was like talking to an old friend. And now, three years later, we have a friendship that I believe will last the rest of our lives. On Day Six, when Sarah talks about "Friendships That Heal," I have no doubt she's talking about us!

    When Sarah and I met, it was the direct result of a difficult time in my life. One she'd been through before. There were times I sincerely wondered how I would put the pieces back together, and I was angry that I had to do it at all. I had been wronged, and it wasn't my fault. I was raw and alone, and it was the perfect recipe for a lot of the self-righteous anger that Sarah discusses on Day Fourteen. It is so easy to lose control of the righteous anger we feel about the wrongs we experience...to go from feeling a quiet conviction that God's will has been violated to suddenly experiencing seething rage because *our* will has been violated. But regardless of the exact situation, people are wronged every day. No one should be treated disrespectfully; and in a perfect world, no one would be.

The problem is: we don't live in a perfect world. We live in a fallen one. God has given us the gift of free will, and that means we can make choices for ourselves, good and bad alike. There are always extenuating circumstances, and every person who wrongs another feels that they have some reason or excuse to do so at the time. *Father, forgive us, we don't know what we're doing!*

There were many times that I thought by holding on to a record of transgressions against me, by keeping score - if you will - I was somehow holding other people accountable. Instead, by holding those grudges so tightly, I was keeping myself from moving past the anger and bitterness I was feeling. And despite my best effort, being angry wasn't hurting the person who had wronged me! Instead, it was hurting me. Feeling so angry all the time made it hard for me to feel happy, to be engaged and loving to my children, and to even begin to move past everything that had happened.

There is more than one school of thought when it comes to forgiveness, although this book attempts to prove one of them wrong. Some people believe that forgiveness is a gift given to the transgressor…that when someone shows remorse or has somehow made up for their mistake, that they can *then* be forgiven as a reward. There are certain conditions to be met before someone deserves forgiveness. If we believe that, then it follows that some people do *not* deserve forgiveness. When talking with people who believe this, I often hear some variation of "Why would you forgive that person? They don't deserve it, after what they did!"

There is another school of thought, however; that the act of forgiveness isn't really about the transgressor, but about the person who was wronged. Making the choice to forgive even when there is no remorse or even acknowledgement of wrongdoing tends to be more challenging and harder to understand. Forgiving unconditionally can be tough to swallow; especially when pride rears its ugly head.

I, like Sarah, had a good reason to remain angry. So do most people, at some point in time. But one day, I woke up and I realized that my anger was affecting me more than the person I was holding a grudge against! So I made the choice to forgive, regardless of whether or not it was deserved. Of course, I would have to make that same choice to forgive many more times before all was said and done. It's a commitment to a process, to a journey, instead of a one-time decision, to give up our perceived control of punishing that other person and leave them to God alone. But every time I made the *choice* to forgive, it got easier.

It wasn't until I chose to forgive *unconditionally* that I realized how much better I felt and what a weight had been lifted off my shoulders! Choosing forgiveness has changed and enriched my life in ways that I never would have imagined. It wasn't about getting the outcome I wanted; instead it was a heart change that helped me in every area of my life. I hope that this devotional will help you along the way to your own heart change.

Sarah and I have many things in common. Our love of the Lord, of our husbands, and of our children are the things that formed our initial bond. But beyond that, both Sarah and I have a strong commitment to coming alongside women who are struggling and who may be feeling alone. We know the bitterness, anger, and feelings of isolation that so often accompany life's trials. We are standing, still, to say this to anyone who needs to hear it:

I have been there. You can survive this. I have hope for you.

-Ellyn McCall
Parenting and Family Life Blogger at ProfoundlySeth.com

# Introduction:

*We are not the bitter ones; we are not the world-worn gossips. We know who we are, and we know that no weapon formed against us will prosper unless we let it. We are daughters of the King of Kings. We are loving. We are loved. We are lovely.*

When I began blogging my story, about four years ago, I knew that forgiveness was at the root of everything I was writing. I didn't know how little I understood about the process or how much my willingness to forgive would be tested over the next several years. Nor did I fully appreciate the gravity of the biblical commands to forgive. I simply knew that forgiveness trumped bitterness and brought about a peace that I desperately needed. I knew that God was allowing me to walk out an eternally significant path. As I sit here now, a single mother for the third time, I feel I have walked the journey of a lifetime in a fast-forwarded amount of time. It is an honor to share that journey (or the portion I have walked so far) with you, now.

Many people have *much* more to forgive than I do. Some may feel that they have less. Because all wrongs committed against us pale in comparison to our sin against a righteous and radiant God, quantifying our pain does not need to interfere with our process of forgiveness.

It is for this reason I've included a few of your stories (names and identifying details changed) in this offering of mine. The issues are different in each of our lives, but the pain—the groaning of humanity—is the same throughout.

And so is the way *out* of that pain.

Our tears fall for many reasons. Whether your tears have fallen over molestation, adultery, the loss of a child, bad business dealings, a broken home, gossip, etc., He has seen it all. He's caught every tear you've cried, and He is eager to take your pain and to heal your unforgiveness.

Whether you choose to read these pages in a few sittings or over the course of the next thirty-one days, please know that I am praying for you. I'm honored to take you with me on this journey through the powerful Word of God—to seek and to find God's heart. I believe with all *my* heart that this is a journey to perspective, to strength, and to loveliness.

# Day 1: Where Time Hasn't Healed, Search Me

Like many old adages we accept as truth—almost as gospel—simply because they've rung steadily in our ears since our childhood, we believe that time will heal our pain and therefore our bitterness. *It has to! Life has to get better than this!* If you've committed to turn through these pages, I'm committed to dissolution of the lies that may be holding you just shy of true freedom. I'd like to turn all worldly, so-called-wisdom on its ear and demand that it submit to Christ. In doing so, may I first boldly suggest that time heals *nothing*?

Healing does not have to take a long time. We may boldly ask the Physician for *instant* healing. Then, as He carefully molds us, we can patiently trust Him with the length of the process.

It is up to us; it is up to Him!

No, healing doesn't have to take a long time—nor does time itself promise healing. Furthermore, time not submitted and surrendered to God creates bitter, drawn-mouthed pessimists who are made old long before their time.

When I was a child we had one of these women on our block. Looking back I realize she was relatively young, her house wasn't haunted, and if approaching her door to sell cookies you would *probably* come back alive.

Her lawn was overgrown and her house looked abandoned even though everyone knew she was in there. She was intimidating, unapproachable, *unloved*. To this day I wonder what happened to her. Who had disappointed her? Who didn't love her back? To a child, the fear that had overtaken her was fear-inducing.

One summer afternoon my brother and I sat sifting through our large pile of gospel tracts and talking about the neighborhood. In our minds, we were great evangelizers. Proving the unquestionable worth of babes' mouths, my brother adamantly concluded, *"She just needs Jesus."*

When you're a child, the answers are simpler…and often truer. We had yet to find a cure more successful than Messiah. We searched frantically through our stack for tracts dealing with loss, grief, and fear. Once we'd found a few that we deemed appropriate, we biked the little ways to her house and then crept stealthily onto her lawn. Uncut trees shaded the entirety of her yard ensuring darkness on the brightest summer day. Her mailbox was all the way up by her darkened front door; my heart pounded in my chest as I lifted the creaky lid while my brother slipped the tracts down inside.

*Then we ran like mad and peddled away!*

Sometimes, like the bitter woman six houses down, we shut ourselves away from the world and *wait* for the pain to subside.

*Tick. Tock.*

Sometimes we end up as the neighborhood outcast in the process.

Bitterness grows like thorns, and soon no human being can get through. Perhaps no one wants to try. Time heals pain? No…it allows open wounds to fester. Time withers. Time wrinkles. Time decays. Who is there to heal our hurts if they are only left to *time*?

Are you aware of the thorns of unforgiveness that have grown thick between you and your Healer? Do some remain that are so well-watered, and possibly "justified," that you walk around them daily without ever acknowledging their presence? These are the things God so desperately desires to reveal. He longs to prune them back and rescue us from the clutches of bitterness, unforgiveness, and pride.

Please don't trust time to take care of your pain; let the Healer lead you through it. Do not sanction your own bitterness (no matter what has happened); He heals to the very depths of our souls!

To begin a life-long walk in, and continually toward, healing, we follow the example of a man who sought God's heart.

The Psalmist David asked God to search him:

*Search me, O God, and know my heart: try me, and know my thoughts:*
*And see if there be any wicked way in me, and lead me in the way everlasting.*
*- Psalm 139:23-24*

Was there bitterness in him? Unrighteous anger?—David wanted to know about every thorn. Following David's example, take a time-out today. Get alone with God in a hot bath or on a walk through a secluded place. Simply ask Him to search your heart for those hidden things; and as they come to mind, write them down.

More and more thorns may be exposed over the following weeks. As more are revealed, keep adding to your list. Keep this list in a safe, private place; we'll deal with it at the end of our journey.

*Father, please search my heart for the bitterness and unforgiveness that hides there. I want to be yours, wholly and without hidden sins or thorns of unforgiveness. I do not want to run from you because of the wickedness in my own heart. Please light a candle to it all, and lead me in the way everlasting.*

_____

_____

_____

_____

_____

_____

# Day 2: As Many Times as They Ask

Within the Body of Believers, there should be apologies. We swim in an ocean of grace, diving in and rising up drenched—ideally both in the accepting *and* in the offering of forgiveness. No Christian should choke on the words, "I'm sorry." Acknowledging the fallibility of our flesh should be as natural as relishing the perfection of our Savior. Sadly, many Christians are waiting for repentance that will never come, and apologies that will never reach their ears, because they have refused to rebuke the sin.

Rebuke. Repentance. Repetitive forgiveness.

*Take heed to yourselves: if thy brother sin, rebuke him; and if he repent, forgive him.*
*- Luke 17:3 (ASV)*

Over and over again.

*Then came Peter to him, and said, Lord, how oft shall my brother sin against me, and I forgive him? Till seven times? Jesus saith unto him, I say not unto thee, until seven times: but, until seventy times seven.*
- *Matthew 18:21-22*


We've all been wounded, and we've all done the wounding. Without any warning to those around us we can walk as ticking bombs—activated by our own pain to release untargeted blasts of destruction. This is the flesh's reaction, not the Spirit's. When we have been legitimately wounded by the sin of a brother, we must not skulk away and allow the offense to fester.

The merciful act of confronting sin in a fellow believer is not so that we might hear an, *"Oh, I'm so sorry I've wronged you!"* If your brother or sister is sinning against you, they are more accurately sinning against God. Rebuke is for their repentance, not for your comfort. Few excel at or embrace the idea of confrontation, but it is something we've been commanded to do.

Rebuke. Repentance. Repetitive forgiveness.

~~~


It was with this command in mind that I sat in the back of a crowded church service with a near stranger whom I'd just asked the question, *"Can I talk to you for a minute?"* I shook from head to toe. I can't confront someone over the phone without it being embarrassingly obvious that I am trembling—the phone rattles loudly against the rings on my fingers, my teeth chatter, and I'm suddenly cold—but face-to-face is a thousand times worse!

I knew what I had to do and the hard words I had to say. Her flirtatious ways, and the mixing of fellowship with sex, were ruining her life and others'; they were threatening mine. God had not only told me to confront her, He'd asked me to lead her into fellowship with Him. Initially, I had been far less than thrilled at the prospect.

For the first few weeks I'd chosen the path of the prophet Jonah. Instead of compassion, instead of mercy, I'd decide to hate her and hitch-hike to Tarshish [Jonah 1:3]. But there I sat, humbled, covered in fish bile [Jonah 1:17 – 2:10] and ready to speak what was in God's enormous heart for a woman who was as much God's daughter as I was.

My words are not always welcomed, even when I am certain God led me to speak them. At thirty-three, I still sound a little like Minnie Mouse. When I open my mouth I simultaneously brace for nods and smiles or some other friendly dismissal. Maybe it's because of the many times I have been rejected that I still feel the urge to fight when God asks me to speak.

Thankfully, I've also had the privilege of being received—of planting fruit-bearing seeds where someone else has plowed and watered. In my late teens I trained as a midwife. I've experienced that sweeping joy of watching and assisting squirming, gasping newborns from womb to breast. Still, no privilege on this earth can compare to that of planting His Word and seeing that seed immediately send down roots and begin to sprout. That is what happened in the back of the church as this stranger became my sister.

Twenty minutes into our conversation you would have thought we'd been friends since childhood. We wept and shook and laughed in each other's arms. She asked for forgiveness for the sins that had impacted my life, and I repented before her for not speaking when God had first asked. I'd come eager to forgive her that day, and she told me through honest tears—admitting she'd needed me and wishing I'd spoken sooner—that she forgave me for my sins, too.

Rebuke. Repentance. Repetitive forgiveness.

A repentant heart is an essential attribute of a Christian; though when we stand in expectation of repentance, without first offering rebuke, we are acting out of turn. How many offenses remain on your "mad list" without the offending party either knowing or understanding the biblical implications of their actions?

*Father, please give me the courage to rebuke sin, in love, when my brothers and sisters sin against me. Please help me to desire their repentance (for their sake). Help me to stand ready and eager to forgive them.*

# Day 3: What Satan Means for Harm

The longer I walk with God, the less sure I am that I can claim a favorite passage of Scripture. So many different legacies and truths have jumped out and grabbed me when I needed them lest I fall. The story of Joseph, though, has stayed with me throughout. Many of my life's philosophies come from his life and the beautiful character of God that his story reveals.

In Genesis chapter fifty, something amazing happens.

Joseph…

…the bratty little brother who knew God made him extra special.
…the brother whom all but one wanted to kill.
…the brother who was sold into slavery as his older brothers sat and ate lunch.
…the brother who spent years in jail after being falsely accused.
…the brother who missed a lifetime with the father who had adored him and given him such a big head in the first place.

Joseph. That Joseph? He was now second in command in Egypt. He held the lives of his brothers in his very hands, and no one would have questioned him if he'd killed them or made them his slaves.

*But Joseph said to them, "Don't be afraid.*
*Am I in the place of God? You intended to*
*harm me, but God intended it for good to*
*accomplish what is now being done, the*
*saving of many lives.*
*- Genesis 50:19-20 (NIV)*


Joseph came to understand something that many believers today do not. He learned through his own life, even before it was written down as Scripture, that God works everything for the good of those who love Him [Romans 8:28]. Joseph loved God. He walked in His ways; he kept God's commandments. Joseph understood that God had allowed his brothers to turn against him in order to accomplish something infinitely greater than sibling harmony ever could.

We see the climax of Joseph's story as he looked back over his miraculous life through the all-knowing eyes of his Creator. In that moment when his repentant brothers stood before him, do you think that Joseph felt pain? When he remembered that day in the cold, dark well—betrayed and abandoned—as the family he longed to call out to mocked and laughed at his misfortune, do you think a tear still welled in his eye?

I've entered those doorways, and experienced those moments of revelation, where the pain from my past is merely the thing that makes Satan sorry—the bigger the mess, the bigger the miracle. Once Joseph realized that God had given him his boyhood dreams, not just to reveal to him the future but to actually *cause* it to happen, I think he must have laughed to himself. That laughter brought tears of its own; but as Joseph stood before his brothers, dripping with jewels, feeding and forgiving them, I believe that grief was the furthest thing from his heart and mind. Suddenly his sadness made sense. Joseph knew, more than anyone alive in that moment, that he served an exciting God. How honored he must have been to have been included in the plan!

Sometimes we wait for the revelation of God's plan in His tangible, recognizable blessings. Joseph's time in prison wasn't pretty; it was dirty...he was hungry. Still, God planned—preordained—to use him there. If Joseph had waited for God to use him until that time when he felt exalted or blessed, God would never have exalted or blessed him.

What happened to Joseph's heart between chapters forty-four and fifty of Genesis? Why, in chapter forty-four, was there lingering bitterness in this righteous and exalted man? And then where did his bitterness go? I believe that though Joseph was living God's plan, he still didn't truly see it. Joseph had yet to be fully convinced that it was *God* who authorized his path through cruel valleys and up this high and unlikely mountain. Once he could see the top side of the tapestry, instead of the mess of strings below, whatever anger, unforgiveness, and sorrow remained simply lifted and floated away.

Where has God taken you in your life that you would not be if someone had not chosen to harm you? How has He transformed your mess—or the mess that was imposed upon you—into a message of His power and grace? Have you permitted God to weave a masterpiece of your pain, or do you only offer up to Him your triumphs? Our God is a masterful artist, and even the things Satan means for our harm become vibrant threads in God's hands.

Ask God to reveal to you His heart. He *always* intends to take our failings, veering, and wounds and to use them for His glory—and He always will if we let Him. Ask Him for excitement, and trust Him with the plan.

*Father, please give me your vision for my own hurts and victories. Please reveal to me the ways you desire to use me in your plan, and let the excitement of being used by you far outweigh any temporary pain.*

_____

_____

_____

_____

_____

_____

_____

_____

_____

# Day 4: Whatever is Pure, Nothing That's Not

Quick, whatever you do, do *not* think of a bright pink elephant! Oh, now you're thinking of nothing but? That's the way our minds work! God knows this; He created our minds.

The Bible commands us to be people of purity and peace—to dwell only on that which is lovely. God doesn't place this demand on us to cause frustration (the opposite is true); but peace, purity, and loveliness are hard to find in the world today. Simply deciding to *not* think negative thoughts is rarely, if ever, a successful strategy. When we manage to shut out the world, and the lies that come through physical hearing, Satan ravenously desires and tirelessly seeks after the *inner* workings of our minds.

Our enemy is formidable; to destroy us from the inside out he needs little more ammunition than our own painful, and painfully twisted, memories...plus a few imaginations thrown in for good measure. Philippians chapter four reveals the biggest obstacle we will face in our path to forgiveness: our human thinking. Rather than tell us what to *stop* thinking, Scripture tells us what we *should* think.

*Finally, brethren, whatsoever things are true, whatsoever things are honest, whatsoever things are just, whatsoever things are pure, whatsoever things are lovely, whatsoever things are of good report; if there be any virtue, and if there be any praise, think on these things. Those things, which ye have both learned, and received, and heard, and seen in me, do: and the God of peace shall be with you.*
*- Philippians 4:8-9*

This passage in the book of Philippians is our counter attack, if you will, against the mental torments of the enemy. Our God knows about the schemes of the enemy. He knows exactly how Satan flusters, worries, upsets, and pulls the rug out from under us completely. He has not left us unprepared!

*Rejoice in the Lord always: and again I say, Rejoice.*
*- Philippians 4:4*

Starting in verse four: we *must* praise Him! If I talk to my mom on a bad day, the first thing she will ask is, *"Is there praise music playing?"* She understands that every second our hearts do not sing to Him is a moment lost and an opportunity for the enemy found (and he *will* prey upon every opportunity to gain an entrance into our lives). In all things, through all things, despite all things, we must live to rejoice in our salvation.

*Let your moderation be known unto all*
*men. The Lord is at hand.*
*- Philippians 4:5*

According to Strong's, the Greek word translated in the King James Version as "moderation" (and in the NIV as "gentleness") is more often translated "gentle" or "patient". I like this better. When I think of gentleness, "effortlessness" is the next word that springs to my mind. A patient person, a person not striving in a world that orders us to strive, *will* be noticed. Our Lord is ever present. He is close enough to reach out and touch—close enough to save our souls, to protect our bodies, and to transform our minds. With this assurance of His presence our unshakable peace, and steady walk, should be strikingly apparent amongst a dizzy and unsettled world.

*Be careful for nothing; but in every thing by prayer and supplication with thanksgiving let your requests be made known unto God.*
*- Philippians 4:6*

Lastly pray, pray, pray. Please do not think that, because God knows the outcome, we are required to lock our worries and concerns in a place of trusting silence. Through verse after verse the Bible reiterates God's abhorrence for whining and complaining, but the constant communication He so desires with us is not limited to gushes of praise. His ears are always open to our hurts. He wants us to communicate our desires. He wants a relationship with each of His children; so talk to Him, constantly, about every detail of your life. Do you think you can wear out the omniscient, omnipresent God with your desire to communicate with and be known by Him? I dare you to try!

*And the peace of God, which passeth all understanding, shall keep your hearts and minds through Christ Jesus.*
*- Philippians 4:7*

When we praise Him, when we rest and trust in the closeness of His presence and talk to Him all day long, we will find ourselves in possession of indescribable peace. It's not something we will wonder about or search for; the peace of God becomes the thing that keeps us—that cradles us. To walk in this peace is to walk within a spiritual barricade of protection. With our hearts and minds guarded from the constant barrage of Satan's arrows, we will have the presence of mind to embrace those thoughts that will further envelope us in His peace.

*Finally, brethren, whatsoever things are true, whatsoever things are honest, whatsoever things are just, whatsoever things are pure, whatsoever things are lovely, whatsoever things are of good report; if there be any virtue, and if there be any praise, think on these things. Those things, which ye have both learned, and received, and heard, and seen in me, do: and the God of peace shall be with you.*

*- Philippians 4:8-9*

Because our thought-life determines our spoken words, and our spoken words bring to life our actions, Satan will not cease to attack our minds. Whether we've tripped into a puddle of bitterness or slipped nose-deep within a cesspool of anger, the way out is always the same. Praise changes our thinking; it turns us from the problem and brings us face-to-face with the loveliness of God. We can return again and again to verse four, lifting our eyes from the pit, and opening our mouths to praise Him, even many times in a day.

*Father, help me to focus on your blessings and goodness. Help me to keep your beauty at the forefront of my mind. Thank you for never leaving me! Keep Satan far from me, and help me to rest in your perfect peace.*

---

---

---

---

---

---

---

---

---

---

---

# Day 5: What I Really Deserve

*For it is by grace you have been*
*saved, through faith —and this is not from*
*yourselves, it is the gift of God— not by*
*works, so that no one can boast. For we*
*are God's handiwork, created in Christ*
*Jesus to do good works, which God*
*prepared in advance for us to do.*
*-Ephesians 2:8-10 (NIV)*

Let's think a minute about what we deserve. I know that many of us don't look at ourselves in the mirror every morning and say, *"Wow, I was bound for destruction before He saved me!"* But if you are a human being, a descendant of Adam, you were born in such a state as required rescue from an inevitable hell. There was no hope for you or me; then, Jesus—Yeshua.

We're born; we sin. In fact it's pretty much the first thing we're good at. The best among us are far from good enough. The standard set by God's goodness is *nothing short of holiness*. Understanding this truth, we must accept that there are only two ways to be saved from death: one being to keep all of God's laws (no one but Yeshua has accomplished this), and the other being a gracious and unearned propitiation by a Savior.

When we're basically law abiding, there is a human tendency to forget that our salvation was not merited; it was not credited to us because of our goodness. When we walk in the holiness we are empowered by His grace to walk in, we may begin to expect blessings to be *paid* to us. When we walk uprightly and someone still chooses to wrong us, we're shocked. We shouldn't be shocked. Still, we may find solace in the sympathetic outrage of others. It's not uncommon for even strong Christians, maybe especially those who have garnered others' respect, to find themselves surrounded by well-meaning supporters.

*"Dump the fool!" they'll cry.*

*"Be angry, you should be!"*

*"Take them to court!"*

*"It's not your fault; you played no part in this!"*

And our favorite, the one Satan has used since the mysterious lie first worked on him, is *"You deserve so much better than this."*

No one should be surprised at how easy it is to climb aboard this fast moving train of comfort. Satan knows which buttons to push and that place on our backs to stroke. He loves to rile us over what we "deserve" and what we are legally "entitled" to have. We are *in* the world, but it's our God who made it and has access to every dollar, every resource, and every good thing. Our enemies' abundance or lack has no bearing on God's ability to bless us. Every good gift is just that—a gift. His welcomed attention is not a payment; it is a blessing.

You may be facing a trial in which the pain and loss are in no way your fault. It *is* possible to be the victim without having played a part, but innocence in a matter does not make one innocent. Denying your identity apart from Christ is a dangerous slope toward bitterness. The wonderfully freeing fact is this: you too were sentenced to death and are as guilty of breaking His laws as is anyone else on earth! We are *all* sinners. We are all either saved by grace or in need of salvation—and we all need grace, either way.

Every day, through every wrong, our response to pain should never be, *"Save me, I don't deserve this!"* So instead, let your heart say, *"Thank you for saving me from what I do deserve. Please help me and keep me through this trial."*

*Father, thank you for saving my soul! Let me see myself through your eyes and through your blood—but as nothing, and deserving of nothing, apart from you.*

_____

_____

_____

_____

_____

_____

# Day 6: Friendships That Heal

*Do not make friends with a hot-tempered
person, do not associate with one easily
angered, or you may learn their ways and
get yourself ensnared.*
*– Proverbs 22:24-25 (NIV)*

In those times in life when we wake and groan,
*"Woe is me!"* it can be tempting to surround ourselves with
friends who do the same on our behalf. These friends are
ruffled and angry over the wrongs that have been
committed against us. They head committees for our
sainthood and spread the news of our innocence far and
wide. They latch onto *our* offenses like raccoons with their
hands around something shiny. They are happy to keep us
riled until our bitterness (inevitably) becomes burdensome
to them. While this can be comforting in the moment, it is
also detrimental to our healing and to the healing of our
broken relationships. Angry friends, by nature, do not allow
us to forgive.

As children, when something is broken we take it to
Daddy and ask, *"Fix it!"* When we're grown, our tendency
becomes to simply throw that broken thing (person,
relationship) away. Surround yourself with people of childlike faith who believe that all things are possible with God
and there is nothing He cannot fix. Because, there *is*
nothing He cannot fix.

People will wrong us, loved ones will leave us, love will bruise us, and time will betray us; but friends who are more interested in our eternal joy than our present, earthly happiness will lift us in prayer and encourage us along the way. Have you surrounded yourself with, or run from, these people? When you slip off the path, is someone there to pull you back onto the straight and narrow? Or are you more comfortable around those who coddle and condone? Someone in your life should be privileged to hold that obnoxious, self-examining mirror; but the only mirror capable of accurate reflection, and then of changing what is reflected, is the Word of God [James 1:22-24].

True friends, sisters and brothers who build our faith and enrich our lives, will not explain away our anger and unforgiveness. They will point us to Yeshua, and away from wrath, even when the unbearable enters our lives.

That's what I watched Mary do for her own daughter just hours after her three week old grandson passed away in the night. Humbled, and more than a little shaken, I stood feet away in silent awe as she placed one hand on either side of her freshly grieving daughter's damp and swollen face. "How could this have happened?" was the inaudible but collective cry. We knew to become huddled bundles of brokenness, standing over covered dishes that no one would have the appetite to eat. At that crucial point when we stood on the precipice of pain, overlooking lapping waves of anger and numbness, righteousness began to rescue. Tears streamed from my eyes as I heard Mary prompt in the kindest of whispers, *"Say it. You need to say it."* She was asking her shell-shocked daughter to praise the Lord!

*The righteous shall inherit the land, and dwell therein forever. The mouth of the righteous speaketh wisdom, and his tongue talketh of judgment. The law of his God is in his heart; none of his steps shall slide.*
*- Psalm 37:29-31*

The righteous are not misled by their circumstances. Good, kindhearted people can find themselves in a place where their own grief, hurts, and experiences (even experiences they have only witnessed) are how they predict the outcome of others' lives. But the righteous…they speak only the words of God. While many will play God—throwing away the promises of His Word and replacing them with the doctrines of their own experience—the righteous walk by faith, not by sight.

While those friends who seek to comfort us with the world's wisdom are well-meaning, they set us up to *not* expect from God. They're afraid we'll get our hearts broken if we put too much hope in the foolishness of faith. Believing they are acting for our good, they are ambassadors of doubt. While God will not force us to trust Him, when we do not expect, we *do not* receive! To place any limitation on God's desire and ability to rescue is to mock the fullness of His perfection and power; mockers are toxic to faith.

*Blessed is the one who does not walk in*
*step with the wicked or stand in the*
*way that sinners take or sit in the company*
*of mockers, but whose delight is in the law*
*of the Lord, and who meditates on his law*
*day and night.*
    *– Psalm 1:1-2 (NIV)*

When we trust that God is good, we see goodness in all that He does. When we trust that He is powerful, we watch in expectation through the darkness of night. When we surround ourselves with people who *insist* on viewing life through the lens of God's Word, we water hedges of protection that surround our hearts and minds.

*Father, help me to love righteousness and*
*surround myself with righteous people. Help me to*
*love all of your ways and to make friends of those*
*who rest in your promises and power.*

_____

_____

_____

_____

_____

# Day 7: Pray, Not Slay

*But I say unto you which hear, Love your*
*enemies, do good to them which hate you,*
*Bless them that curse you, and pray for*
*them which despitefully use you.*
*— Luke 6:27-28*

Are there any words from Scripture that are more controversial, or outside our human mind, than these? By very definition, friends are for loving and enemies are for hating. But even the world can do that! The Holy Spirit need not apply.

One of my older twins first faced the reality of this lesson when she was only four years old. It was a cold winter day, and we'd taken the family to a fast food restaurant so the kids could run off some steam in their play area. Yards of plastic tubes are just about their favorite thing in the world. Most of the tubes are opaque— red, green, or yellow; but there are a few places where the plastic is clear. The kids always stop in those sections to wave hello and to make sure we're still watching.

It was the middle of the afternoon on a weekday, so we had the place pretty much to ourselves. Truthfully, I prefer it that way, but my children (at least the four who weren't infants at the time) possess none of my often crippling introverted nature. When a grandmother, mother, and young daughter joined us, our crew saw a welcomed friend. The little girl was cutely dressed with ribbons in her hair. She made our four look like orphans from the 1940s. They invited the princess to play, and soon they all disappeared together within the maze.

For a few happy minutes, the entire room echoed with shrieks of joy and laughter. I smiled and sank deeply into something sugary and caffeinated while my husband and I cooed at our youngest. I was proud of my children's welcoming sweetness and was having a "good Christian mommy" moment. But when I looked up to locate a scream and saw that three year old princess straddling my daughter, biting her shoulder, and pulling her hair, "I'm a Christian" was suddenly the furthest thing from my mind.

I yelled for the mother, and we called for our children. She didn't believe that her daughter was capable of the horrors I had just witnessed—and I was old enough to not fight with strangers. We all sat down to eat our burgers in silence, and I rocked my crumpled and sniffling daughter in my lap.

Mothers tend to hold their children's offenses just a little tighter than do fathers, and I held both my daughter and her wounds in my fiercely mothering arms. As we finished our last bites of burgers, though, and I began to wipe down the table, I glimpsed an expression on her face that looked a little too much like anger. Desiring to help her out of the pain (now entirely emotional at this point), we nudged our daughter as the Holy Spirit nudged us, *"You need to go tell her you forgive her."*

She was reluctant, but she made her way off my lap and to the neighboring table. *"I forgive you,"* was all that she said, softly but very sincerely. The little girl's mother looked up and then quickly away, as if something written across our four year old's forehead was shocking and maybe offensive. Her daughter lapped up the forgiveness bringing to my mind a malnourished puppy, and her grandmother looked on and smiled.

We prayed for them, and we asked God to abundantly bless their lives. Still, for weeks afterward, the pain of that trauma would resurface for our tenderhearted daughter. *"Mommy, remember that time..."* was heard daily for awhile. Satan attempted to trap her as he's done so many times with me. In the late afternoon, as she'd lie on her back on the living room floor and allow her mind to wander, Satan would relentlessly remind her that she'd been wronged. *And oh, how wronged! She'd done nothing; she'd been loving...and still, she had been attacked!* So we'd stop, and we'd *practice* the Christian walk until the torments no longer came. We prayed blessings for her tiny enemy; we prayed again and again and again.

Satan seduces our masochism. He seeks to drug us with self-righteous anger. If you've fallen victim to his schemes, if your internal dialog is filled with angry, what-I-wish-I'd-said conversations, pray. Where anger would have you curse, bless. Where pride would have you run and hide, stay and serve. Satan brings our enemies to mind as a weapon against our souls. He stirs the cauldron of our minds—but we don't have to let him. Yeshua calls us to love as He loves.

Do you have a mental list of those you'd like to hurt, slap, or maybe simply avoid? Write those names down and form your new prayer list. Ask God to reveal the ways you can minister life into your enemies' lives.

*But love ye your enemies, and do good, and lend, hoping for nothing again; and your reward shall be great, and ye shall be the children of the Highest: for he is kind unto the unthankful and to the evil. Be ye therefore merciful, as your Father also is merciful.*
*-Luke 6:35-36*


*Father, bring those people whom I have hated to my mind. Show me how to bless them and pray for them. Teach me to see them and love them as you do.*

_____

_____

_____

_____

_____

_____

# Day 8: Do Justly. Love Mercy. Walk Humbly.

*Sing to God, sing in praise of his*
*name, extol him who rides on the clouds;*
*rejoice before him—his name is the Lord.*
*A father to the fatherless, a defender of*
*widows, is God in his holy dwelling.*
*God sets the lonely in families, he leads*
*out the prisoners with singing; but the*
*rebellious live in a sun-scorched land.*
*— Psalm 68:4-6 (NIV)*

"The rebellious live in a sun-scorched land." As a lover of cool weather this verse is hauntingly descriptive, and particularly poignant, to me. It reminds me of Jonah sitting alone under the hot sun because he willingly despised the umbrella of God's authority. Have you ever wondered how it was possible for that righteous man (the one who had just been vomited by a large fish) to sit haughtily on a hill and wait for the fireworks of damnation?

Jonah hadn't run from Nineveh because he was afraid for his own safety. He knew that God was more than able to protect him. No, Jonah ran from Nineveh because he was afraid God intended to use him to show His great mercy to the sinful Ninevehites...and Jonah was right.

God used Jonah as His mouthpiece. Because of Jonah's reluctant obedience, the lives of over one-hundred and twenty thousand people were saved from judgment. Angels rejoiced; but Jonah loved justice—not mercy. While *sin* requires punishment, God provides a way for *sinners*. Without acknowledging both the *law* and *grace* aspects of God's personality, we are in rebellion against His heart.

Who, from verse six of Psalm sixty-eight, are dwelling in a sun-scorched land? These rebellious are whom God is unable to defend and protect—He won't force us. They fight against God's ways. The God who longs to father His wayward children sits back quietly while they insist on their own doctrines and their own traditions—their own way.

I tell my children, in the many times a day I hear bickering from them, *"Come to me. Come to me! If she looks at you funny and it makes you sad, you can come to me! You should tell her you are wounded and ask her to be kind, but do not return the stare. Do not pick a fight. If she doesn't listen to your words, just come to me. Talk to me, and I will handle it. I will defend you....but if you decide to handle it, I will handle you."*

Like their mother, my children love justice...justice for the crimes committed by others, I mean. When I refuse to punish their repentant siblings for some sort of treachery against them, how quickly my home is filled with Jonahs. They're unhappy with the unrighteousness of their siblings, they're suspicious of their repentance, and they're even more upset with me.

*But to Jonah this seemed very wrong, and he became angry. He prayed to the Lord, "Isn't this what I said, Lord, when I was still at home? That is what I tried to forestall by fleeing to Tarshish. I knew that you are a gracious and compassionate God, slow to anger and abounding in love, a God who relents from sending calamity. Now, Lord, take away my life, for it is better for me to die than to live."*
*– Jonah 4:1-3 (NIV)*

Mercy is God's very nature. He is slow to anger. There is no one who is so far down the path of unrighteousness that God would not accept his repentance and forgive his sins. If this angers us, if this causes us pause or pain, we must examine our own walk with God.

*He hath shewed thee, O man, what is good; and what doth the LORD require of thee, but to do justly, and to love mercy, and to walk humbly with thy God?*
*-Micah 6:8*

*Father, help me to trust you with my enemies. Help me to walk in humility and with justice, and give me a heart full of mercy. Please keep me from rebellion against your ways, and lead me to safety with singing.*

_____

_____

_____

_____

_____

_____

_____

_____

_____

_____

_____

_____

_____

# Day 9: Exercising Your Mind

*Therefore, I urge you, brothers and sisters, in view of God's mercy, to offer your bodies as a living sacrifice, holy and pleasing to God—this is your true and proper worship. Do not conform to the pattern of this world, but be transformed by the renewing of your mind. Then you will be able to test and approve what God's will is —his good, pleasing and perfect will.*

*- Romans 12: 1-2 (NIV)*

The question I am most often asked in regard to forgiveness is, *"How do you stop thinking about…?"*

*Fill in the blank with whatever plagues you.*

I do have an answer to this question, but I have to admit that it often frustrates me to give it. The answer is hard. The answer begins a process. The answer involves exercise.

I used to hate exercise. I wasted so much time searching the deep recesses of the internet for that miracle pill that would flatten my post-twin-babies tummy without subjecting my body to trauma. I eventually submitted and came to the conclusion that there is simply no such thing.

*No pain; no gain—and the same is true with our minds.*

Our minds are truly spectacular places full of all manner of mystery. In fact, there is no way for one man to truly know another, in my opinion, because we are not able to read each other's minds. But our minds should be pure; that's the goal. We should not be ashamed to walk down the road wearing neon-red brain-interpreters as hats. Our thoughts should proclaim the peace of the gospel of Christ. Our minds should be empowered by the gospel! While there is nothing biblical about being in denial (the opposite of truth), the Bible is very clear about what we should be thinking. Is it hard to avoid thoughts of betrayal, hatred, rejection, or fear? Of course it is! When these thoughts come, we must exercise our minds; and like all exercise, the hardest part is forming a healthy habit.

Christians are commonly discouraged and deceived by their own thoughts:

I think [rotten things] therefore I am [rotten].

If we are Christ's, we have the mind of Christ [I Cor. 2:15-16]—though we are not always utilizing it. We need to be aware, though, that the barrage of thought that storms our minds is not exclusively God's. Neither are our thoughts only our own; our enemy also speaks. Because Satan is the Prince of the Powers of the Air, negative thoughts *will* come.

*And you did he make alive, when ye were dead through your trespasses and sins, wherein ye once walked according to the course of this world, according to the prince of the powers of the air, of the spirit that now worketh in the sons of disobedience;*
*- Ephesians 2:1-2 (ASV)*


As children of God, we have power over these thoughts.


*Finally, brethren, whatsoever things are true, whatsoever things are honorable, whatsoever things are just, whatsoever things are pure, whatsoever things are lovely, whatsoever things are of good report; if there be any virtue, and if there be any praise, think on these things.*
*- Philippians 4:8 (ASV)*


We have the power, and the right, to take every thought captive. We are called to make—*forcibly demand*—them to obey our Lord!

*Casting down imaginations, and every
high thing that exalteth itself against the
knowledge of God, and bringing into
captivity every thought to the obedience of
Christ;*
*- II Corinthians 10:5*

It is not the initial thinking of a contrary thought that is sin; sin is the ongoing dwelling on that thought. These thoughts do not originate from within us. Still, Satan seeks to enslave us with the negative things we think and feel. If we believe that our sinful thoughts are ours, if we own them, we will cave to them. We will welcome them into our hearts and speak them with our mouths.

*"How do you stop thinking about fill-in-the-blank?"*

As believers in a Holy God, and those who bear His name, we must recognize the need to stop sinful thought processes. This is probably the most important step, as many believers do not realize the power their thoughts have over their lives. The secret sin of a negative (lustful, hateful, ungrateful, fearful, complaining) thought-life is not pleasing to God, and it will lead to negative feelings and behaviors. We must learn to label each thought at the moment it enters our head.

*Hello thought, are you from God? Oh, then by all means, come in!*

*Hello thought, are you from Satan? Sorry, no entry.*
*Delete.*

While I find no Scriptural evidence that Satan can hear our thoughts, I also believe that he knows quite a few of them. Remember, he can put them there! When we think something we do not or should not believe (i.e. *"My children are in my way," "I'm not in love with my spouse," or "I'm too busy to stop."*) we must first identify the thought as evil. The deleting of that thought comes by way of strategic action.

My response to these detected thoughts isn't showy or time-consuming. I simply say, or whisper if the situation calls for a whisper:

*"Praise God!"*

It's that simple; at least I'm arguing that it is. It takes no time out of my day, although I have had people look at me strangely in the grocery store.

When the enemy puts a thought into *my personal head*, I believe that said spirit watches and waits for the impending turmoil and self-destruction. If an opposing reaction is not witnessed, it has proven much more common for the assault on my mind to continue.

*And continue.*

When I stand up and fight—*"Dear Lord, that does not line up with your Word and I do not believe it! Please take it away! Would you? Praise God!"*—that's the delete key. With continued use and consistency, our minds become renewed.

On our path to forgiveness, Satan will bombard us with painful memories, thoughts of betrayal, feelings of guilt, and self-righteous hypocrisy. At first, rejecting a thought might not be as simple as pressing a key on a keyboard; but with enough exercise, we can truly train our minds to repel those thoughts that are not of God. If we are in Christ we have the spiritual obligation, and the power necessary, to replace those thoughts with what is good, pure, and lovely.

*Identify. Delete. Replace.*

It's a never-ending process for old-bodied humans, but it will get easier in time. If Satan is stealing from you by way of your thought-life, there's hope. There is victory in Yeshua.

*Father, teach me to discern between your voice and the voice of my enemy. Help me to be sensitive to your voice, and teach me to reject anything contrary to your Holy Spirit.*

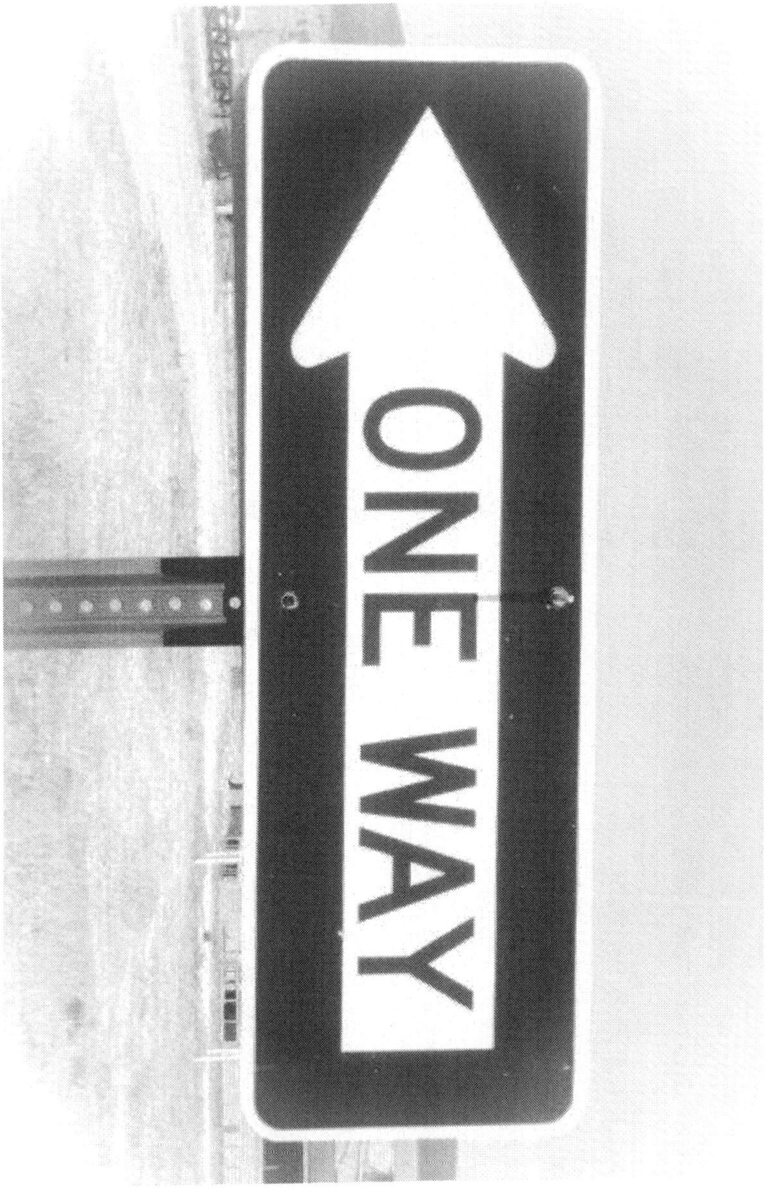
ONE WAY

# Day 10: Looking Ahead

*By faith Moses, when he had grown up, refused to be known as the son of Pharaoh's daughter. He chose to be mistreated along with the people of God rather than to enjoy the fleeting pleasures of sin. He regarded disgrace for the sake of Christ as of greater value than the treasures of Egypt, because he was looking ahead to his reward.*
*— Hebrews 11:24-26 (NIV)*

Sometimes, maybe oftentimes, we're not only bitter because of what someone has done to us but because of what they've been *allowed* to do. We think they've gotten away with something. They sinned; we didn't. Although the resulting emotion is debase—filthy, we must recognize where we're jealous.

When jealousy presents itself as the result of another's sin, we need a heart change as much as the person who has sinned against us. We are no longer looking ahead. In order to flee from sin, we must grasp its nature in such a way as would prevent any other action but our turning in disgust. In order to embrace holiness without the stumbling block of attractive sin, we must stop sugarcoating and glamorizing what slips and sneakily slides off the straight and narrow. Putting lipstick and diamonds on a corpse will not prevent it from rotting. *Every single sin* brings forth slavery—and eventually death. Repentance heals; scars remain. While He is faithful to use our scars, nothing can replace the joy that comes alongside us, and encourages us, in our faithful obedience. There is no counterfeit emotion that rivals the peace in a friendship with God.

Looking ahead, instead of claiming the rights to happiness *now*, does not make sense to the world. Faith looks a lot like foolishness. My husband Brian and I are currently separated (as we've been two other times before). Recognizing our need for a do-over I have acknowledged death where there *is* clearly death, but I will not stop looking ahead—in hope.

True and tested faith stands still and hopes beyond all reason. When our earthly strength is drained from our bodies, when our flesh dies and submits to the power of new life, and when our mortal eyes are dimmed in the light of His glory…that is when His strength, His will, His reality can live. By its very definition, what is fully real is largely intangible this side of eternity. As Christians, we always have the promise of *more*, so we are looking ahead to the more.

Many have balked at my desire to reconcile with my husband. They express their disappointment with words like, *"He's off having his fun, and you're...not."* That very statement implies that he is out sinning, and then it calls the sinning "fun".

*But now being made free from sin, and
become servants to God, ye have your fruit
unto holiness, and the end everlasting life.
For the wages of sin is death; but the gift
of God is eternal life through Jesus Christ
our Lord.*
*-Romans 6:22-23*


Slaves to sin are *not* having fun; do not be deceived into viewing sin in the same twisted way that the world does. If Christ's mercy has allowed you to escape a certain sin, if His grace has sustained you to withstand a particular temptation—rejoice! With every step toward life and away from death—rejoice!

In Christ, sorrow only lasts for the night; joy comes in the morning! Slaves to sin are on the opposite clock, and it's mourning that comes with the day's light. Until we fully accept this truth, we will merely see sin as something we are not permitted to do: pleasurable and forbidden. We'll be teenaged Christians who are inwardly itching to rebel— whether we ever do so or not.

No, sin is not what we are cruelly kept from. It's what we were freed from; it's what we are saved from! Those who have not allowed Christ's blood to break their chains of sin are to be pitied and prayed for. Hell should be stormed and ravaged on their behalf. They are never, ever to be envied. Those who deeply know Him, and have fully embraced their cross, have no doubt of this. Peace reigns in the lives of the righteous, and those who lack the freedom they have in their Savior are envious of that peace.

Are you jealous of the world, or is the world jealous of you? Allow God to work in your heart and mind and give you the eternal perspective needed to chase His life with passion and disdain those things leading to death.

*Father, show me the reality of sin, and help me to be truly grateful that I am no longer a slave to unrighteousness. Give me joy in the freedom I now have to serve you, and give me peace no matter what others around me are choosing.*

---

---

---

---

---

---

---

---

---

---

# Day 11: Skinless

*Put on the whole armour of God, that ye*
*may be able to stand against the wiles of*
*the devil. For we wrestle not against flesh*
*and blood, but against principalities,*
*against powers, against the rulers of the*
*darkness of this world, against spiritual*
*wickedness in high places.*
*– Ephesians 6:11-12*

In our house, we believe in the word "hate". It sounds harsh when coming from a two year old's mouth— and it is—but I believe in teaching my children to love the things that God loves and *hate* the things that God hates.

Our only true ally is God, and our only real enemy is Satan. When my oldest daughter saddles up beside me and asks, *"Mommy, why do you really think that Daddy doesn't want to be married?"* I feel no obligation to worldly wisdom. I offer up not a wishy-washy scoop of post-divorce psychology, but something biblical—steadfast and eternal. I can honor my husband *and* my God. I swallow hard, and then without anger toward her father or shame toward me, I put the blame where it truly belongs. *"I think that the Devil has been talking,"* I whisper, gently touching her teachable ears; *"I believe that it's God, and obedience to Him, that keeps people in love."*

I know she's learning these lessons when she responds, *"Mommy, remember when I said I wanted to marry Davey?"*

*"Yes."*

*"Well, I don't think that's a good idea anymore."*

*"Oh?"*

*"Yeah, I want to marry someone who's being taught about loving God while they're a kid,"* and then she throws in for good measure, *"I really hate the Devil."*

Some of us might dislike peanut butter, but we hate lies—or we know that we should. A few of us might disregard blue in favor of pink, but we hate Satan. Hate what He hates; love what He loves! At the top of God's love list is the world, not the spirit of the world, but the *people* of the world. We're called to *love* people as Christ does. And we're called to *hate* sin.

God warns us about our true enemy because he is skinless; we cannot see him. As fleshly beings with five senses, we understandably find it difficult to operate outside of the physical realm. Things invisible to our perception are easy to ignore. Satan uses this little weakness to rip our lives apart. How? Because we don't know who or where our real enemy is. He creeps around like a lion before daybreak while we are distracted by *minor* enemies with skin.

~~~

Gayle is a long-time reader of my blog, and I can relate to almost every aspect of her testimony. When

Gayle's husband was seduced by an old gambling addiction, she could have taken the path that many of her friends and family members recommended—and they were quick to recommend a divorce. His gambling was destroying the family and stealing the security of their children. While Gayle did choose to separate from her husband, she never saw him as the enemy.

In fact, Gayle continued to love and prayerfully serve her husband. For over a year, Gayle worked two jobs because he was unable to provide for them. She spent many nights interceding for her husband's freedom while sprawled across the living room floor with a box of tissues as a pillow. Gayle knew who her enemy was; she knew that he was skinless. She yelled at *him*, screamed at him; she was angry at him for seducing and capturing her husband. She asked Jesus for mercy for her husband's life and soul. The enemy wasn't going to get away with stealing the head of her family— not on her watch!

Satan did not and cannot make Gayle's husband sin, but he often presents a tempting offer. Our enemy is not weak or ignorant; he has been a shrewd study of human nature since the sixth day of creation. He knows what will tempt us, and he will not even offer what will fail to turn our heads.

Who has wronged you after first being captured by a debilitating addiction or obsession? We have all fallen prey to the enemy's lies at one time or another. Maybe moving your fleshly enemies from the "offender" column to the "victim" side will give you more insight into how to pray for them.

When we stand up to our skinless enemy, we are happy to see our earthly enemies blessed. We delight in their freedom; we pray for their release from the curses placed upon them by the one enemy common to mankind. We trust that our earthly enemies will be brought to justice (we trust God with them), and we hope mercy and redemption for them (we pray for them). There is a place for your hatred, just make sure it's not aimed at skin.

*Father, make me a warrior, and teach me to battle the enemy without distraction. Help me to separate my hatred for sin from my love for people, and help me to see both through your eyes.*

# Day 12: Not Tossed

*Consider it pure joy, my brothers and sisters, whenever you face trials of many kinds, because you know that the testing of your faith produces perseverance. Let perseverance finish its work so that you may be mature and complete, not lacking anything. If any of you lacks wisdom, you should ask God, who gives generously to all without finding fault, and it will be given to you. But when you ask, you must believe and not doubt, because the one who doubts is like a wave of the sea, blown and tossed by the wind. That person should not expect to receive anything from the Lord. Such a person is double-minded and unstable in all they do.*

*– James 1:2-8 (NIV)*

James speaks of life's trials because there is simply no way to avoid them. Though we will face many trials in our lifetime, if we let them, they will work to perfect us. Trials make us patient; they build our courage and our faith. When we learn to submit to, and joyfully embrace, the inevitable fruits of hardship…we're made wise.

In chapter one, James presents a circular point: Trials make us whole and wise; but if we lack the wisdom to walk out life's trials in the way we have been called to—with joy—the Bible says that all we need to do is ask for that wisdom. If we ask God, and if we believe Him for wisdom, He will grant it; He will teach us how to walk in it. There is a catch, though; further trials will be involved in the teaching!

Those times of proving and teaching are the reason for James' warning against doubt. We are warned to ask for wisdom without doubting that God will grant it. If we waver, if we take our eyes off of Yeshua and fret about the test, if we question whether the trials are working for our perfection, we'll soon begin to bob and drown. No one knows more about drowning in doubt than Peter:

*"Lord, if it's you," Peter replied, "tell me to come to you on the water."*

*"Come," he said.*

*Then Peter got down out of the boat, walked on the water and came toward Jesus. But when he saw the wind, he was*

*afraid and, beginning to sink, cried out,*
*"Lord, save me!" Immediately Jesus*
*reached out his hand and caught*
*him. "You of little faith," he said, "why*
*did you doubt?"*
*- Matthew 14:28-31 (NIV)*

Some days we sail on smooth water while the sun gently warms our face. We're in a seaworthy vessel, and Yeshua is right there with us. We're in love with Him; we see Him clearly. With our eyes on our Savior, we're eager to offer forgiveness to those who have wronged us; we're excited to pray blessing for them! These days are a welcomed respite from the trials and tribulations in life, but just remember: In this life we are *promised* trouble! When Yeshua calls us out of the familiar safety of our fishing boat, and when the wind stirs the water, turning its glassy top to white, choppy waves…what will demand our focus? Will what wins our attention in these times be faith in our Savior, or will it be the waves?

I've been there amidst waves that crash so violently my attention is pulled downward to them. The sinking is nauseating; the swirling and drowning—hopeless! Have you ever felt yourself drowning in doubt? In these perilous moments, our water-logged memories of Christ's face are not sufficient for saving what is left of our faith. We need to see Him! And while we could simply *look up* and find Him, we can become too disheartened by the waves to even try.

In James we learn of God's purpose for trials: The Father uses them to make us perfect and wise; we're warned against allowing Satan to use them: He uses them to steal our purpose. Bitterness and offense are ways our enemy stirs the waters, and he does this in all of our lives. Satan works tirelessly to draw our attention from Yeshua. God has a holy purpose for our trials and for our wounds, and He will reveal that plan if we let Him.

When we set our minds to becoming undistracted people of forgiveness, we determine to fix our eyes upon Yeshua. To counter our obedience and thwart this plan, Satan swells waves of doubt all around us. With our eyes upon the waves we will mistrust the very goodness of God. We will question whether our hardships are capable of producing good fruit. When we ask for the wisdom to love and to forgive, Satan will focus his attack on our belief in redemption—on our faith for healing; he will attempt to drown our hope in thoughts of doubt.

*"All things are possible…except this."*

Our God loves us with the fierce devotion of a perfect mother and a blameless father; He wars for us violently and cradles us lovingly in His arms. If He commands us to forgive, as He does consistently throughout Scripture, He will not leave us powerless or only limitedly able to do so. But we must believe Him! We must block out the world's ways and ask for God's. We must trust that the trials are working for us and at the same time ask for the wisdom to walk them out. That victorious walk on water is achieved only through stubborn faith! If we believe Him despite the weather, we will maintain peace— and avoid sea sickness—at the same time!

*Father, I believe you. I believe all of your promises are true. Please grant me wisdom to live my life according to your will. Give me joy in all of my trials, because I believe each time of testing is making me wise.*

---

_____

_____

_____

_____

_____

_____

_____

_____

_____

_____

_____

_____

# Day 13: Does Your Life Preach the Gospel?

*And he took the cup, and gave thanks, and gave it to them, saying, Drink ye all of it; For this is my blood of the new testament, which is shed for many for the remission of sins.*
*– Matthew 26:27-28*

Sinners who reach upward and unabashedly accept the unearned gift of salvation are granted sainthood through the blood of Yeshua. It is only because of Yeshua that the Father can look upon us and seek a relationship with us. After this miracle has taken place, we can begin to walk as saints. Although the transforming of our life is a process, that process should continually proclaim the renovating power of the unparalleled grace of God. Does your life, specifically the way you see and relate to others, reflect this transformation? When you're offended, and pain puddles around your toes, do you glide over it, wade through it, or fall on your face and drown? Do you drink deeply of the cup of Christ's sufferings or become distracted with planning your defense? When others observe your life, do they glimpse the powerful work of the gospel?

Since the beginning of creation, God has demanded blood for sin. We don't have to understand it; it's just the way He works. Until Yeshua, the sacrifice was foreshadowing. No lamb, goat, or turtledove was pure and spotless enough that his blood could appease God's wrath, but they pointed Israel toward THE LAMB—the promised Messiah. It is the only the begotten Son of God whose blood is so pure and so awesome it can cover, no, wipe from memory, the sins of everyone who has ever lived. And we have new a High Priest in the Heavenlies (the risen sacrifice Himself) who administers this blood on our behalf.

I have accepted the sacrifice that Yeshua made for me. He is the gateway of this narrow road I walk down. This does not mean that I do not sin, but it certainly means that I do not embrace sin. I have chosen the straight, the privileged, the road of the few. My heart and my desires are for God; I want to love the things that He loves.

Of course I am a hypocrite of unending proportions. My heart is wicked in ways I don't even know. But because I stand in the shadow of what He did, because I have committed my will and my walk to be continually transformed to the will of my Holy God, God fellowships with me and calls me perfect and righteous. He sees me, His adopted daughter, through Yeshua. I've been accepted, and I'm being transformed, by the purifying blood of His Son.

If you have chosen Him, this is how He sees you, too. He desires that *all* men come to Him and that *no one* should perish. So, that is how we should endeavor to see the whole world as well.

*You are the salt of the earth. But if the salt loses its saltiness, how can it be made salty again? It is no longer good for anything, except to be thrown out and trampled underfoot. You are the light of the world. A town built on a hill cannot be hidden. Neither do people light a lamp and put it under a bowl. Instead they put it on its stand, and it gives light to everyone in the house.*
*-Matthew 5:13-15 (NIV)*

Unless we're alone in the middle of nowhere, there are very few times in our days when our actions are not affecting someone's soul. The way we drive, the way we treat our waitress, how many items are in our cart when we pick the "express" lane, what we post online, the expression on our face, how we dress, and whether we pay our bills on time are all being thoughtfully scrutinized by an unbelieving world. Though I'd argue that nothing is watched more closely than our ability (or lack thereof) to *freely* offer the forgiveness we claim was abundantly shown to us. Do we, or don't we, believe in His power to clean up a life? Do we, or don't we, believe in His power to make brand new?

It's all about preaching *Him*.

We like to say that *He would have died just for me* (or you), but He didn't die just for me (*or you)*. Christ's blood was poured out for the forgiveness of His Bride. Unless you agree with its work for others, how can you prove its work in you?

*Father, please help me to glorify you and represent you with my life. Help me to preach the gospel by the way I live, and especially by the way I treat those who have sinned against me.*

---

---

---

---

---

---

---

---

---

---

---

---

# Day 14: Righteous Versus Self-Righteous Anger

*Be still before the Lord and wait patiently for him; do not fret when people succeed in their ways, when they carry out their wicked schemes. Refrain from anger and turn from wrath; do not fret —it leads only to evil. For those who are evil will be destroyed, but those who hope in the Lord will inherit the land.*

*-Psalm 37:7-9 (NIV)*

We're called to hate sin—not to dislike it, but to ascribe to it a passionate, nose-turning, heart-groaning hatred. So how are we to react to the wickedness that seems to flourish all around us? How do we avoid the confusion that comes from watching our earthly enemies succeed—from watching sin work for the good of those who love it? We know to focus our anger on sin and Satan; we know to pray for our enemies. But how are we to accomplish this task when everything in us cries out for *justice*?

We must sit still and wait patiently; we must trust that God is much more interested in, and able to bring about, justice than we are. When we fully trust the Lord's integrity we fall in line behind Him and gain all of the strength of the winning team. Our perspective is eternal, and the result of that perspective is peace...

*When we're angry at sin and Satan.*

Even with the very best intentions, though, that sneaky shift from righteous to self-righteous anger can easily happen. It might be so subtle that we cannot even detect it, but it culminates in *"How could they?" "I would never!"* and other such log-in-eye sayings. Oh, how these thoughts lead us to sin!

April and David's first year of marriage is a prime example of Satan's stealthy seduction to self-righteousness; because whether friend, family member, or spouse, self-righteousness blooms on the vine of another's sin.

April married the man of her dreams, and because of a mighty work of God she is still married to him today. For the first year of their marriage, though, she was sure she had made a mistake. David didn't care for or comfort her like he had when they were dating. He romanced her, married her, and then failed to lay down his life for her (like many young husbands do).

When someone's sin affects us in the way David's affected April, it's almost impossible not to notice. We have the privilege, though, of gently handing that sin to Yeshua. He'll take it. When we hold it too long, Satan begins to ask in incessant whispers, *"Why are you the only one righteous?"* and our self-righteous thoughts began to grow. Before the end of their first year of marriage, April had given into these communions with her enemy by justifying an emotional affair.

*Do not fret—it leads only to evil.* Focus on the sins of others, and sin will follow you around!

~~~

Understanding the principle of righteous versus self-righteous anger is so very important to our journey of forgiveness. It was during an especially difficult moment in my life that God chose to show me the baseless and ugly nature of *my* self-righteousness—my own fretting and worrying over *others'* sins. For that I am so grateful! God doesn't show us our sin to shame us. If there was no hope for change, He would surely hide our faults and permit us to live in blissful ignorance.

I'd received the kind of news that I'd rather hear in private, so I ran to the only place I could be alone. As I paced back and forth in the empty church bathroom, I recounted every wrong done to me and all of my reasons for rage. In an instant stirred up an all-encompassing hopelessness and anger where peace had been just moments before. Just as Yeshua reached down and pulled Peter from the lapping waters, God grabbed me by the hand. Then he whispered something that would turn me to Him and toward forgiveness. He said, *"Never forget this feeling."*

I never have.

There is a self-righteous high that comes over me when I succumb to that dip in the cesspool of "justified" rage. I plan my brutal tongue-lashing knowing I can slice through thick skin when I aim to. My hope is no longer in God, and my anger is no longer directed solely at the things that enrage Him. When my spiritual defenses are down or weakened, this feeling can overtake me more abruptly than a crashing wave.

In that moment, alone in the church bathroom, the wave swept ceiling to floor. My heart raced, boiling my blood. I felt powerful and sick. My neck and shoulders stiffened and my head began to pound. This time, though, in this eternally weighty moment, God spoke loudly enough to be heard over the heady sound of blood rushing by my ears.

*"Never forget this feeling. It is not from me,"* and I responded with an, *"Uhh, oh...well, duh!"*

Righteous anger has nothing to do with our innocence; it's about God's holiness. I had turned my back for just a split-second to admire my own goodness in the mirror; but by focusing on the sins of others, I lost sight of my own inheritance from Adam. Seizing the opportunity, the Devil ran away with my peace!

It is not simply mankind that stirs our anger. It is not just our spouses and friends whose betrayal can cause us deep pain. Sometimes the one we are so mad at is the very One who saves! We live in a time when fellow Christians allow, sometimes even encourage, us to be angry at our Creator. *"Be mad at God, He can take it!"* as if God's ability to hold up under the weight of our disappointment has any bearing on our anger being right or wrong. When we dare to be incensed at God, we remove ourselves from the answer and instead side with the problem. In its most detrimental form, anger at God will forever damage the way we view our loving Savior. In its most innocent presentation, it is simply a waste of our time. When we trust Him, we view all of life based on the understanding that God will not do us harm. And through this insight, we find peace.

God *can* take our anger; He can bear it, but anger toward Him is always misplaced. If it is permitted to fester, unforgiveness toward God Himself is one of the most common reasons that people turn from righteousness and instead go the way of the world. The only anger that profits is the kind that agrees with the heart of God. Anger that elevates us or our human ideals gives the enemy room to roam.

*Father, please help me to remain calm and trusting as my enemies succeed and prosper around me. Help me to pray for them, and help me to trust you with them.*

_____

_____

_____

_____

_____

_____

_____

_____

# Day 15: Do Good to, Pray for, Bless

*"You have heard that it was said, 'Love your neighbor and hate your enemy.' But I tell you, love your enemies and pray for those who persecute you, that you may be children of your Father in heaven. He causes his sun to rise on the evil and the good, and sends rain on the righteous and the unrighteous. If you love those who love you, what reward will you get? Are not even the tax collectors doing that? And if you greet only your own people, what are you doing more than others? Do not even pagans do that? Be perfect, therefore, as your heavenly Father is perfect.*
*- Matthew 5:43-48 (NIV)*

I've heard it said that one should pay careful attention to how many times a principle is mentioned in Scripture. If God says it once, He means it; if He says it more than once, He wants to be sure that we really get it. If we heed the insistence of Scripture, we will be thoroughly convinced—beyond reason and without question—that we *are* required to love our enemies. God is not taking their side over ours; He's asking *us* to side with Him. We've already died and been reborn! The strength to walk a righteous life is offered post-mortem; we have no right to apply the same standards of righteousness to those who have yet to die. Alongside our salvation we received the command to love. In newness of life we receive the *power* to love. This love, like all real love, has practical application: do good to, pray for, bless.

~~~

When Samantha married Drew, divorce was not a door she left open. Even after years of abuse, she kept it closed. Samantha understood that God changes and transforms; her faith was not easily deterred by Drew's hard-hearted resistance. But in a saving move, God cracked a window. In an effort to bring safety into her life and the lives of her children, Samantha packed their belongings and left with her heart.

The next few years were, in ways, even more difficult than the previous had been. Drew took his anger out on the children; and, before a judge, he blamed the abuse on Samantha. Samantha tip-toed around bitterness as her life rocked from side-to-side.

In time, both Drew and Samantha met and married other people. While Samantha's marriage brought joy into her life, Drew's marriage meant that another person was now critiquing her parenting and interfering in the lives of her children. This is not what she had planned for them, and bitterness threatened to grow.

Praying women do inexplicable things. Samantha's heart slowly lost its hardened shape—molding instead to the will of her Father's. He'd asked her to bless her enemies, and she believed Him. Passive prayers soon gave way to bubbling brooks of blessing. For her ex-husband and his new wife, she prayed that they would recognize themselves as abusers and be healed from the deep roots upward. She prayed that they would have a flourishing relationship with her children. She prayed for their marriage; for the man who had been incapable of loving her, she prayed that he would love the step-mother of her children. There were no prayers for punishment or vindication. Everything she prayed for her own marriage, Samantha prayed for Drew's. And as she prayed, God mediated terms, facilitated peace, and healed hearts in the way only He can.

~~~

When you pray, what do you ask for your own life? What do you need from God? Are you struggling in your finances, or are your children straying from Him? Are your relationships crumbling? Is your body or your mind in need of healing? Do you need more time with Him, more focus, more energy, more vision? Do you need more of the Holy Spirit—more grace—to overcome a sin or an addiction? Are you repentant for your sins? Do you need to grasp God's immeasurable and inexhaustible forgiveness?

Many of these most likely apply, and other needs may come to mind. Write out a personal prayer asking God for both the eternal and the earthly things that you need. You can trust God with your needs *and* your desires. Ask Him to come through for you and to break those chains that still need to be broken. Ask Him for *every* good gift that He has for you in His timing.

Then take a giant leap of obedience. Once your letter is finished, write out an identical copy on behalf of everyone on your "enemies" prayer list. These are not the things that we instinctively pray for those who have most deeply wronged us; but we must allow God to teach us how to pray. Yeshua came to set the captives free. As His children, we are not only *recipients* of this freedom; our prayers and desires for others should reflect an outpouring of His mercy and grace.

*Father, teach me how and what to pray for my enemies. Please answer my prayers for them, and let their freedom and blessing bring me joy!*

_____

_____

_____

_____

_____

_____

_____

_____

_____

_____

# Day 16: The Devil Almost Made Me Do It

*Let no man say when he is tempted, I am tempted of God: for God cannot be tempted with evil, neither tempteth he any man: But every man is tempted, when he is drawn away of his own lust, and enticed. Then when lust hath conceived, it bringeth forth sin: and sin, when it is finished, bringeth forth death.*

*– James 1: 13-15*


It was the fall of 2006, and I sat in what I'd later dub "the meeting of angry wives." A tear-stained woman ranted about the porn blocker on her computer, and a consensus of disgust thickened the air in the stifling room. She wanted her husband to be a man, and everyone seemed to agree. He shouldn't need protection from the Devil; she was tired of the Devil getting so much credit. All he needed to do was *man up.*

It was as simple as that.

*"I think he is being a man,"* I squeaked and then coughed as I rocked a car seat with each of my feet. *"He's being a fallen man, and he's asking for help."*

In situations like this, I regret opening my mouth approximately 99.987% of the time; this time was no exception. All eyes were soon on the "new girl". In a room packed with wives who had become victims to all manner of sexual addiction, I still had joy; I still loved my husband. Most of them were sure that I'd come around.

*"I get mad at Brian for bringing home fudge,"* I more confidently but still quietly continued. If everyone was going to stare at me, I might as well have something to say. *"If something goes wrong in my day, I am going to eat that fudge! If I asked my husband to put a padlock on the junk food cabinet, I don't think he'd make fun of me."*

Almost everyone related to my confession about the junk food, but few equated the vileness of a food addiction to the sickening addiction to porn—and in consequence, perhaps it's not. It is what we turn to instead of turning to Yeshua, though; those are the things Satan dangles. Anything, Satan will do *anything* to keep us from falling on our faces and admitting defeat before our Redeemer. He knows how high Yeshua lifts the humbled, and he knows those things that will keep us from bowing low.

Judging strictly by the e-mail I receive, more of my blog readers are angry over pornography than any other topic. They should be angry! Satan is using pornography to ravage our sons, to make impotent our husbands, and to steal at least a little self-worth from an entire generation of women. In the midst of our righteous anger, though, we have to stop being so self-righteous!

I believe in taking full responsibility for my poor choices (even pain-induced reactions such as eating an entire tub of frozen whipped cream on one of the worst days of my life). But in what I can only define as primal moments, my option of *choice*, my free-will, is sometimes indiscernible. It is not until the moment of guilt that I consistently recognize my own foolishness.

When we're wounded, and we fail to kneel before our Father with that offering of pain, we're left clawing at the walls and desperate for comfort. Satan offers the ready-made kind. Although he rarely makes us bow to reach it, this worldly succor will eventually take us lower than we ever thought we could go.

Yeshua is the lover of our souls; Satan is the soul's seducer. If seduction was not, by very definition, almost undetectable, we might walk securely though blinded and unprepared. Because this is not the case, we must continually be on guard.

~~~

Not three years later, in early 2009, I sat pregnant and happy, though tired and consumed by the details of a wearying day. One light burned brightly in my kitchen ceiling, and a moth circled madly around it.

It's not as if I'd never seen a moth meet his maker; I'd been morbidly entertained by the cracklings of a bug zapper as it secured the lawn on a hot summer night. Still, I knew there was something in this moment that God wanted me to witness; entranced, I continued to watch.

The dizzy moth drew up slowly within the beam and momentarily disappeared inside the fixture. After a second or two, he made his escape like a rocket reentering the atmosphere, grateful to have survived a death by fire. I looked on as he continued swirling and diving as if controlled by a force other than his own mind—plunging down to safety and then pulling fiercely back into the radiating rays.

Each time he would enter the fixture he would stay a second longer. I found myself cheering him on, wondering how his delicate wings were withstanding the intense heat of a seventy-five watt bulb. "Come on, you can do it," I whispered, as he lingered one last time.

*He couldn't do it.*

I sat dumbfounded, wondering if he'd tried to escape that last time. After all, I had watched him do it three times before. I knew it was possible. Had he simply grown too tired to flee, or did the warmth of the bulb seduce him until the very moment that it burned him alive?

*"Why did you want me to see that?"* I groaned. A moth had died; yet a tear tumbled inexplicably down my cheek.

For those of us watching from a place of victory, we're tempted to shake our heads and roll our eyes at those still drawn toward death. But I sat still for hours that night, thinking about a moth. As I talked with my Father, He gave me revelation and imparted to me His mercy for those enslaved and seduced by the enemy.

No matter how Satan has tempted us, and with what sin he has lured us, if we're honest with ourselves, we must admit how persuasive he can be. Accordingly, even though we must acknowledge that Satan cannot force our will and make us sin, we feel sorrow for our own sake when he tricks us. Likewise, we should offer each other that same consideration.

*Father, please help me not to excuse my sins while shaking my head at others'. Help me to have compassion on everyone around me, knowing that we share the same enemy.*

_____

_____

_____

_____

_____

_____

_____

_____

_____

_____

# Day 17: Put Down Your Stones

*So when they continued asking him, he lifted up himself, and said unto them, He that is without sin among you, let him first cast a stone at her.*

*– John 8:7*

When I read of Yeshua saving the adulterous woman from impending stoning, I used to think He was breaking His own law. It is God, not religious men, who gave Moses the commandments. The men who stood haughtily clutching stones knew that adultery is not something God takes lightly. It is God who demands holiness, and those who sought her stoning were expecting the cleansing of the Lord. But they were only interested in cleansing *her* sin. They were far less interested in abolishing the sin of the guilty man who more than likely stood among them. They showed no mercy. They imparted no judgment.

As she squirmed in filthy agony, ready either to die or to be born, her arms soaked with tears as she guarded her face, the men who stood above the adulteress did not see her. As they looked upon her brokenness with an only intensifying desire to crush her sin, they lacked the ability to separate what she had done from who she was—from who they were.

What Yeshua did in John chapter eight shook man's feeble attempt at righteousness deprived of sincerity. In a moment foreshadowing His death, and the world's redemption, He leveled the field. He forgave the wandering Bride, and He commanded Her to sin no more. He tore down the bleachers and put all sins and sinners together on the dirty ground. Yeshua looked, as God always looks, at hearts; He commanded the saintly sinners around Him to do the same.

It was the older, wiser men who dropped their stones and headed toward home first. The longer we live, the harder it becomes to convince ourselves that we are righteous or even *somewhat good*. Eventually, though, every man came to the same conclusion. I imagine that standing face-to-face with the Son of God sped the process of realization along.

Wisdom demands that we see ourselves as sinners. It requires that we put our own need for forgiveness far ahead of our quest for personal justice. As we embrace our absolution, we would scarcely trade Yeshua for the protected delusion of our innocence. When we take for granted our pardon, heavy stones make our hands unusable.

~~~

In 2011, I was husbandless for the second time. I still wore my wedding rings, and I spent most of my time loving, praying for, and forgiving my broken husband. A corner of my heart, though, was darkened and cold; and there, at a cozy table for two, hatred and fear had a standing nightly reservation. I welcomed them in the darkness; I fed them, and I poured them wine. As I embraced the power that comes through knowing them, I directed it toward a certain type of woman I was afraid my husband might find, or be found by, in his absence.

Then late one night, as I sat in my lonely bed with a hot laptop on my knees, I read something that (though I hate to admit it now) made me shudder. With shouts of jubilee, a dear friend announced that she'd just led a "stripper" to the Lord. I could not have known that something, anything contrary to the great commission, was sneakily lurking within me like a poison; but the stabbing pain I felt at reading her proclamation was a merciful wake-up call. My reflexed reaction disgusted me. It convicted me. It brought me from quickened anger to a purifying puddle of weeping.

After drying my eyes, I read on that this precious, hatchling believer was in need of immediate financial assistance. Christ's blood had cleansed her heart and saved her soul in one all-encompassing flood; but there was still work for the Church to do. Yeshua insists on action—*uncomfortable action.* I wiped another heavy rainfall of tears as I had the privilege of paying her bill. My hands were once again useful, and I sat healed.

Are your hands full of stones? Maybe you've held them tightly for so long that they feel a part of you now, but it's time to let them go. You will release your grip in the presence of Yeshua!

*Father, please help me to drop all judgments
I have held against others. You are the only one
sinless, and you are the only judge.*

_____

_____

_____

_____

_____

_____

_____

_____

_____

_____

_____

_____

_____

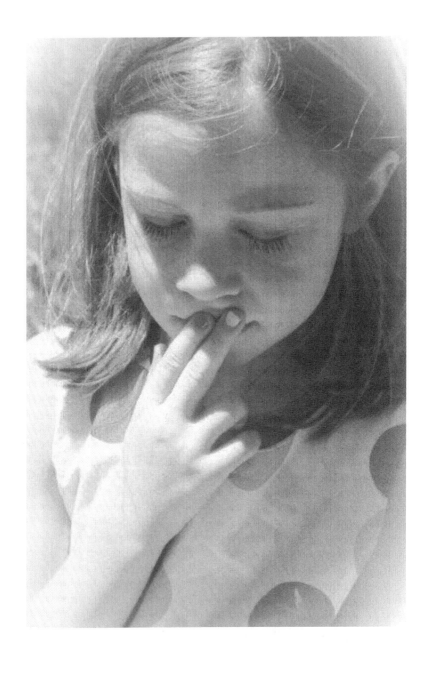

# Day 18: Take Your Place in the Kingdom

*It is not fitting for a fool to live in luxury—*
*how much worse for a slave to rule over*
*princes! A person's wisdom yields*
*patience; it is to one's glory to overlook an*
*offense.*
*– Proverbs 19:10-11 (NIV)*

Proverbs nineteen speaks of princes and slaves and the way that each should live. Do we realize that we are the princes? As sons and daughters of the Most High God, we are royalty—princes in the Kingdom. No longer slaves to sin, we are free! But do we look free? Do we act free? A prisoner may have his cell door opened, but he is not free until he steps out and begins to walk.

Many of us have had our cell door opened with the only key, the one possessed by Yeshua. We've watched Him replace our prison orange with purple robes; we've felt Him place a princely crown upon our grateful head...then we've turned around to continue our conversation with the other inmates. We plan to leave just as soon as we've restored our reputation in the prison. First, there are misunderstandings to clear up, wrongs to right, and lawyers to hire.

*For we know that our old self was crucified with him so that the body ruled by sin might be done away with, that we should no longer be slaves to sin —*
*-Romans 6:6*

Until we claim our place in the Kingdom, slaves (and what they think of us) *will* rule us. Slaves still belong in the prison; we look ridiculous there! The imprisoned *will* mock us. Let them mock us for what we are, not for what we say we are and are not. Let them point and jeer at our peace because it is outside of their natural understanding. Let us not make a laughing stock of Christianity by possessing no more freedom, no better defense, than those in shackles and chains!

When I upset my children by offering their siblings forgiveness in lieu of consequence, I have to turn my head to hide my giggles. I understand their anger! *"God, defend me! I've been so wronged!"* was the occupation of my quiet time for quite a while. I begged God to exalt me and to humble my enemies, to elevate my name as the innocent, and to make my righteousness known.

I know, from brutal experience, that to shut one's mouth, when Satan is doing everything in his power to pry it open, is one of the hardest day-to-day problems that we face. I've had my share of defeats, both in every day conversation and in my blogging. I know the desperation that comes with that internal mantra, *"Please, please! I just want to explain!"* I think this is why Yeshua so beautifully exemplified his lack of defense for us in Scripture.

When Yeshua was accused, He gave no answer [Luke 23]. Like everything He did while on this earth, He did so that we might follow His example. He was teaching us how royalty lives, and princes need not bother with accusations. The King sees all, and anyone who accuses His children will deal directly with Him. Yeshua, even though He was God in all His power, understood that it was the Father's job to defend Him. No defense is more powerful, none holds more authority, than His!

When the world looks at you, do they see a prince or a pauper? Your cell door has been unlocked and kicked open. Are you still standing inside? Some questions shape our lives, so I'll ask what a godly counselor once asked me when I was seeking help and advice regarding my marriage. I had hoped she would excuse my actions; instead she stole my ability to choose any recourse but prayer and submission. She quizzed:

*"Do you trust God to defend you?"*

*Father, please help me to live like royalty! Help me to see the freedom and privilege of my salvation, and help me to walk out my true identity as a prince in your kingdom.*

# Day 19: Thou Shalt Not Gossip

*Whoever would foster love covers over an offense, but whoever repeats the matter separates close friends.*
*– Proverbs 17:9 (NIV)*

Even as a mall-dwelling teenager, the hustle and bustle of city-life was not for me. Today, after more than fifteen years in the mountains, it would take a pretty hefty reason to draw me back. When my five year old dials her play phone, she pauses briefly and then responds to the imaginary voice on the other end, *"Oh, I'm sorry...wrong neighbor!"* I love that my children are growing up surrounded closely by neighbors and friends.

With all of the benefits and safety, though, comes the downside of small town *talk*. Small town people feel a moral obligation to *talk*. Unfortunately, this same small town behavior can also be found inside many churches in the form of gossipy prayer requests.

Eleanor Roosevelt once said, *"Great minds discuss ideas; average minds discuss events; [and] small minds discuss people."* Like my dad says about good sayings that are not Scripture, *"It's not in the Bible, but it's biblical."* When we discuss God, and the things of God, fellowship is at its greatest. Gossip is one of the lowest uses for the spoken word.

It might look like a detour from the topic of forgiveness, but let's return to the subject of friendships. If we are friends with people who gossip, we bring unnecessary strife to our heart and mind. By searching those darkened corners in others' lives, we will face issues of unforgiveness and offense that we should have never been asked to face. Positioned within earshot of a gossip, we will become angry about things we had no business knowing in the first place. If "news" and "stories" occupy our thoughts, we will soon forget that the world's problems are not solved by our worry, but they are better left to God.

To renounce gossip is to embrace a trusting peace. By acknowledging that sin and heartache surround us but it is God who convicts and heals, we're simply refusing to be a part of the problem. When we choose to take what we do hear to the cross and stop our ears from what we should not hear, we put our trust for healing and redemption in God's hands.

Gossip and rumors are perpetuators of a person's past wrongs. People rarely grow beyond the expectations of their family and friends. Gossip often leaves a trail of lasting damage by not allowing a repentant sinner to move forward with Christ. And in the case of current offenses, gossip prevents the covering of an offense with love.

Many believe that if a matter is true, or strongly believed to be true, it may be repeated freely without the stigma of gossip. This is not what the Bible demands. If we accuse our brothers or sisters, we are to do so face-to-face and alone. Spreading matters in the name of confidence or prayer requests not only destroys homes and reputations, but it can and will take the gossiper down in the process.

*Father, teach me to speak the truth in love and to lovingly cover offenses. Help me not to be, or associate with, a gossip.*

_____

_____

_____

_____

_____

_____

_____

_____

_____

_____

_____

_____

# Day 20: Hypocrisy

*"Why do you look at the speck of sawdust in your brother's eye and pay no attention to the plank in your own eye? How can you say to your brother, 'Let me take the speck out of your eye,' when all the time there is a plank in your own eye? You hypocrite, first take the plank out of your own eye, and then you will see clearly to remove the speck from your brother's eye.*
*- Matthew 7:3-5 (NIV)*

When we judge others' sins as more important than our own, our own sins grow until they blind us. Accountability is our safety net against the cold, hard floor of independence; as Christians, we should accept and offer biblical rebuke of sins. However, we must trust *God* with restoration. Others' sins do not exist as a challenge on which to sharpen our own holiness. We are not responsible, or adequate, for fixing our loved ones *or* our enemies.

If we are bothered and distracted by our brothers' and sisters' sins, we are wasting the time God would use to make and mold our own lives. What should instead occupy our time is growth in Yeshua. When our personal pursuit is forgiveness, restoration, and holiness, others will find it uncomfortable to sin around us. We should not be comfortable people to sin around; not due to our judgment, but because where the Holy Spirit is welcomed, He is welcome to convict.

When we drop to our knees, broken and desperate before our Father, there is a higher prayer than, *"Please fix my husband, convict my mother, and change my sister."* Rather, we should cry out, *"Fill me!"* To be part of that wonderful process of conviction, we must be so full of the Holy Spirit that Satan runs from us and sinners run to Yeshua *in* us. It is the Holy Spirit who convicts sinners, and it is Yeshua who saves them; no words derived from within ourselves can accomplish this.

~~~

Rebekah and Ryan were ten years into a difficult and spiritually mismatched marriage before Rebekah allowed God to teach her this lesson—and before either of them began to grow.

They attended church together almost every Sunday, but Rebekah admits to having nagged him there most weeks. It's no surprise he wasn't eager to go. Very few men would enjoy being run-through by their wife's guilt-tipped elbow at the mention of their flaws from the pulpit.

You see, Rebekah loved church because it reinforced her own concerns and desires for her husband's life and soul. Sermons rarely convicted her, because she was always listening for *him.* It's not that Rebekah thought she was perfect and flawless—far from it. But because she saw her husband's sins as more immediately concerning than her own, all he could see were hers.

Rebekah is not alone. She deeply loved Ryan and was genuinely concerned for his soul. The thought of being eternally separated by death kept her wide awake with worry, and she spent many nights in prayer. It took ten years for Rebekah to give her husband to the Lord. So for ten years her witness was ineffective. It wasn't until Rebekah *stopped* worrying about her husband, and instead lived the outward *and* inward life of a Christian, that God began to work in Ryan's life.

If it is your desire to be used in others' lives, ask God to make you more like Him. If we ask Him to remove the planks from our eyes, He will lead us further and further away from sin and toward holiness. He desires to make us like Him, and He loves it when we ask Him these things.

*Father, I want to be used to bring many to you! Please cause others' faults and failures to grow quiet and dim as you lovingly reveal to me my own.*

_____

_____

_____

_____

_____

# Day 21: Through His Eyes

*But, beloved, be not ignorant of this one
thing, that one day is with the Lord as a
thousand years, and a thousand years as
one day. The Lord is not slack concerning
his promise, as some men count slackness;
but is longsuffering to us-ward, not willing
that any should perish, but that all should
come to repentance.*
*- II Peter 3:8-9*

My youngest daughter needs to be heard and seen
much more so than my other children. When another
daughter puts on her dress-up best and then comes and
twirls in front of me, I cannot say, *"You look beautiful!"*
without hearing, *"Do I look beautiful, too?"* My attention
needs to be on her every second. She needs to be my
favorite, and she is! But I have four other favorites, too.

When we're hurting, we forget that our Father has
billions of other children. We need to be His favorite!
Although He has all the time in the world to devote to us,
individually, we can be tempted to ask Him to prove His
love for us by swiftly smiting our enemies.

Just a few days ago, my post bedtime peace was interrupted by a cry from the kids' room. Someone said something rude, and someone else had taken matters into her own hands. It was up to me to sort it out.

*"Why did you hit her with your stuffed animal?"*

*"Cause she was rude to me,"* she answered.

*"Oh, I see. The Bible definitely says, 'If they're rude to you, be sure to get them back.'"*

She bristled just as I do at that first glance of conviction.

*"Well?"*

*"No, that's not what it says,"* she mumbled like reality was severely disappointing.

*"What does it say? Let's see, 'Do not say...'"*

*"'Do not say, I'll pay you back for this wrong.'"* The words came begrudgingly and were almost inaudible to human ears.

*"'Wait for the Lord...'"* I prompted.

*"'Wait for the Lord, and He will deliver you.' But God never delivers me!!"* she whined. I think she wanted God to smack her sister so that she wouldn't have to. At the very least, she wanted me to.

We might be God's favorite, but we should not forget that we're not the only one. Whether our enemies have turned to Him or not, they are His creation and are thusly His children. God is slow to anger, against us *and* our enemies, because He desires that all of His children come to Him. He has time to wait for repentance, and because of His mercy, He takes His time!

When we learn to view our enemies as God sees them, forgiveness for them comes much more easily. Rather than hoping God will catch them and punish them while *in* their sin, we can begin to pray for their healing and for redemption in lieu of punishment. We still want our pain to cease—we long for resurrection, but through God's Fatherly eyes, we want that same eternal joy for all the world.

*Father, thank you for your patience with me. Help me not to take it for granted or forget that I was also in need. Teach me to see everyone through your eyes. Teach me to rest and trust when you extend your mercy to others.*

_____

_____

_____

_____

_____

_____

# Day 22: Stop. Drop. Apologize.

*Therefore, if you are offering your gift at the altar and there remember that your brother or sister has something against you, leave your gift there in front of the altar. First go and be reconciled to them; then come and offer your gift.*
*- Matthew 5:23-24 (NIV)*

As we ask God to remove the planks from our own eyes, He will bring to mind those things we have yet to apologize for or repent of. Even as I began writing this book (*my* gift before the altar), I was required by the Lord to stop a few times and make amends. Oh, how quickly I can forget my own harsh words yet furiously ponder others'. When I allow God to convict me of *my* sin, the sins of my brother lose their hold over me. These shifting realizations must be met with repentance, and repentance takes a first step in apology.

Whether it be pride, forgetfulness, or awkwardness, there are many excuses at our disposal that would keep us from sorrowfully expressing the deep remorse we feel over our sins. Because our apologies have the power to remove stumbling blocks and make smooth the paths of others,

Satan will take many forms to convince us not to make them. While repentance for sin against a brother might seem like an obvious obligation of a Christian, reconciliation also begs for the righting of *misunderstandings* (offenses that are caused by accident or carelessness). The reason for the offense is often not what is most important; the restoration of relationship is.

~~~

We tend to give ourselves more grace than we extend to others, especially during life's harder trials. There are times when the ground around us is hard-trodden dirt, and there are other times when egg shells pave the way. I was in an eggshell season when a dear, out-of-state friend decided to come for a visit. While she was in my care, I was preoccupied with my own secret worries. I took everything she said that could have been twisted, and I wrung it until my hands were sore. As a result, my attitude toward her was far from loving. I failed to make her feel anything but awkward in my home, and at some point I think we both began to count the hours that were left in the week.

Once back at home, she didn't call; I didn't call. Neither of us chose to write. We just let the relationship fall by the wayside, even though it had been an important one in both of our lives. For two years, I made excuses, reasoning that the breakdown of our relationship was both our faults—not willing to humble myself and make things right. It wasn't until God first asked me to write about forgiveness that I knew the topic had to extend to apologies. I reached out to my sweet friend with long-overdue repentance; and because she is gracious, our relationship has been restored.

In the Body of Christ, it is most often fellow Christians who do damage and cause disillusionment—both to brand new and to seasoned believers. Do not let this be your story. Lead others toward Him; don't push them away from Him. Do not offer sacrifice to God without first restoring relationship with any and all you have wounded.

*Father, please bring to my mind any hurtful thing I have done or said to my brothers or sisters. Give me the courage to apologize and the integrity to make amends.*

# Day 23: Wretched, but Forgiven

*This is a faithful saying, and worthy of all acceptation, that Christ Jesus came into the world to save sinners; of whom I am chief.*

- *I Timothy 1:15*

Paul is famous for claiming the title of "worst" and "most forgiven". As a pardoned murderer of Yeshua's followers, he must have felt this beautifully and deeply. While humbly embracing Christ's mercy, Paul is simultaneously urging all of us to accept the title in our own lives.

Our miraculous favor with a holy God should draw those around us to Him. But if we believe we were easier to clean up than our neighbor, God will not use us to reach our neighbor. We must accept our own sinfulness, as painful as the reality can sometimes be. We were not two steps from heaven before God dusted our shoes and welcomed us in. We, like everyone else, had to stand dead center under the gory cascade of His cleansing blood. He had to scrub us head to toe, heart to mind.

The Bible gives us instructions. It outlines the path God demands we walk in order to fellowship with Him. He tells us these things though He knows we will fall. Sin cannot stand in His presence, and He desires *our* presence for all eternity. He longs to cover us with His motherly wings and sit us on His fatherly knee. He does not remind us of our sinfulness out of cruelty…but rather out of love. While continually pointing us to the path of righteousness, He is also mercifully revealing Yeshua.

To know that we are wretched, and yet forget we are forgiven, is what Satan would like as much as convincing us we are good apart from Christ. Both points of view will stunt us, leaving us where we lie—broken. Satan is happy with a hopeless sinner and happier with a useless saint.

I've witnessed many couples like Andy and Maria: he was the sinner; she was the saint. Before Andy would find salvation from his addictions, and freedom from his demons, Satan would take him to a depth so dark it would threaten to chain him there. Andy was fired from his job and publically humiliated for his addiction to pornography. Andy was deeply shamed, and truly sorry, for the vileness of his sin. Forgiveness, to Andy, seemed like a story too good to be true.

While his pregnant wife attempted to remain supportive, Maria faced an ugly trial of her own. She had done nothing to bring this scarlet letter into her life, and the desire to cut ties and run was overwhelming. She was too distracted by her innocence to remember her own forgiveness—until that moment of choice when she fell prostrate before her King. It was this pivotal moment that she shared with me.

The Holy Spirit's sweet conviction held Maria tightly that night; He rescued her from disgust and pride. Only by focusing on her own relationship with Yeshua did she learn to see her husband through the same sacrifice and blood that had cleansed her. God kept her, strengthened and not destroyed, in the marriage. He honored her, and He allowed her to play a part in her husband's healing.

Guilt and shame are Satan's tools, and we should neither accept them nor use them as God's. Though conviction and guilt might look similar at first glance, conviction gives an answer, offers a solution, and invites us to change. Guilt, on the other hand, simply tells us that we are bad. We must know that we are wretched, but we cannot stay there. The sorrow we should embrace is the sorrow of conviction, and it leads us excitedly to change. The sorrow of guilt leads to death.

*For godly sorrow worketh repentance unto salvation, a repentance which bringeth no regret: but the sorrow of the world worketh death.*
*- II Corinthians 7:10 (ASV)*

*Father, I acknowledge that I am the worst and the most in need of your grace. I acknowledge my need for you in all things, and I thank you for forgiving me. Please bring the excitement of conviction to my life, and change me by the power of your Spirit.*

---

# Day 24: Forgiving Yourself

I've taught my children to "repent and flush". They absolutely love the act of pantomiming their sins into the "sea" and then flushing them forever away! It is important for them to know that God truly *forgets*—that they can drop it all under the blood and into the ocean of His mercy and grace. They need to understand the power of a do-over.

They need to understand, and so do I.

Every time I watch their excitement, I learn. I grew up with a tendency to scuba dive for my sins. I dredged them from the bottom of the deep sea just to tell God, *"See?! I'm still sorry."* To make sure He knew that I took my sins seriously, I repented again and again...and again.

The problem with this form of reflection is that it made it very hard for me to see myself as clean. I returned to the scene of the crime to survey the damage, and I continually repeated *the same crimes.* What we think about, we speak; what we dwell on, we become. Our past is only important because it has been and is being redeemed. Our testimony is not about how bad we were, but about how good, how great, our God is!

By denying the power of His blood to cleanse each sin upon confession, we are rejecting His power and denying His grace. The Bible says that when we repent, He removes our sins far from us and no longer associates us with them! The beautiful news about forgiveness is that we are not only commanded to offer it, but it is freely offered *to us.*

*For as the heaven is high above the earth,*
*so great is his mercy toward them that fear*
*him. As far as the east is from the west, so*
*far hath he removed our transgressions*
*from us.*
— *Psalm 103:11-12*


*He will again have compassion upon us;*
*he will tread our iniquities under foot; and*
*thou wilt cast all their sins into the depths*
*of the sea.*
— *Micah 7:19 (ASV)*


If you're like me, you'll appreciate the visual reminder, so take a marker to toilet paper or write on leaves by a rushing stream. Write down your sins, whatever you're currently dredging up, whether you haven't yet repented of it or have repented a million times. Write them down, but don't linger with them for long. Write, repent, and *flush*! Be childlike, and allow God to take your sins all the way to the bottom of the sea. And whatever you do, let them stay there! Don't go searching; go and sin no more.

*Father, thank you for removing my sins far from me! Thank you for your forgetfulness! Teach me to tune out the enemy and to truly embrace my forgiveness.*

_____

_____

_____

_____

_____

_____

_____

_____

_____

_____

_____

_____

_____

# Day 25: Sorry, You Do Not Have That Right

*"Then the master called the servant in. 'You wicked servant,' he said, 'I canceled all that debt of yours because you begged me to. Shouldn't you have had mercy on your fellow servant just as I had on you?' In anger his master handed him over to the jailers to be tortured, until he should pay back all he owed.*
*-Matthew 18:32-34 (NIV)*

There is a parable [Matthew 18:21-35], a story so deep and so moving that it was the first thing God broke through and whispered to me in the darkest hour of my life. He said, *"You do not have the right to not forgive."*

You've probably heard the story; you may have read it dozens of times. I had, but we can numbly read the words without letting them change us. There is always some reason why they do not apply to us.

Except that all Scripture relentlessly does.

You see, there was this man, a servant, who owed an immeasurable fortune to the king. Think of an amount that would be impossible for you to pay sans the luck of the lottery. Think of that amount and triple it. Got it? That's about how much this man owed. Only this man did win the lottery— a pardon from the king! He danced and he sang and he was unimaginably grateful. Can *you* imagine having a debt like that forgiven? I can.

After a little time passed, though, this man no longer saw himself as a debtor. He was blessed and forgiven *and free*! Maybe he told himself that his pardon had been more or less merited, or maybe (in all the excitement of a guiltless life) he forgot how much he had owed. I've seen and can attest to its existence: Christian amnesia is a *very* real thing! Whatever the reason, he decided that being debt-free was not quite enough, and he began to seek his own fortune. First stop: a man who owed him somewhere around a year's wages. It was no small debt, and it was rightfully owed him. When this fellow servant begged more time to pay, the forgiven man refused him mercy. He locked him in a debtor's prison, and he threw away the key.

When the king heard of the unforgiving servant's repulsive deeds, he wasn't simply disappointed. He didn't take into account the size of the debt or how much the forgiven servant might have needed the money. No, he reversed his judgment of mercy; and he, too, threw the unforgiving servant into prison to be tortured for all that he owed.

Your obligation to forgive does not teeter on what has been done to you! It is not weighed according to how much you are owed. Your right to withhold forgiveness was snatched at the moment you accepted the unearned propitiation of Jesus Christ. He is not a cruel God—your pain matters to Him! But if you refuse to have mercy on your brother, God cannot show mercy to you.

*Father, what you did for me through Yeshua removes my right to hold any offenses. Thank you for what you did for me, for releasing me from my prison. Do not allow me to hold anyone else in chains.*

---
---
---
---
---
---
---
---
---
---
---

# Day 26: Forgive and Be Forgiven

*And forgive us our debts, as we forgive our debtors. And lead us not into temptation, but deliver us from evil: For thine is the kingdom, and the power, and the glory, forever. Amen.*

*For if ye forgive men their trespasses, your heavenly Father will also forgive you: But if ye forgive not men their trespasses, neither will your Father forgive your trespasses.*
*– Matthew 6:12-15*

Some of you are waiting on apologies. All you need to hear is, *"I'm sorry,"* maybe coupled with tears. Then you're sure your forgiveness will flow freely. What do you do in the meantime, though? What steps toward forgiveness should you take, what prayers should be prayed, in those days, weeks, years, or decades that come between an offense and an apology? What if the apology never comes?

When Yeshua taught His disciples to pray, I believe He did so with a completed thought. Many aspects of our daily walk are outlined in this simple passage [Matthew 6:9-15]. And in the Lord's Prayer, unlike other times in Scripture, there is no mention of an apology or repentance preceding the forgiveness we are commanded to offer. There is a qualifying statement, though: forgive so that you can be forgiven!

Salvation, if we fully accept it—truly *get it*—will make us grateful people. Like children entering a wonderland, we should skip down this earthly road with heavenly eyes full of awe and wonder. If we understand what we have been given, not a day should pass without a deep sigh and a moment of reverent gratitude. In this state, forgiveness flows from us just as freely as it is accepted by us. This is the life of love we are called to live as Christians.

When we accept the free gift of Salvation, we do so with a repentant heart. We know we have missed the mark, and it is this knowledge that births our freedom. Yeshua does not stand over us with a score card keeping track of our continual failures. Though He commands us to sin no more, love covers a multitude, and His is boundless. God now sees us the way He created us; He's recreating us. He cheers us on accordingly! That is the way we should see everyone else—through our Father's eyes.

God demands that we remain forgiving, because a perpetual state of forgiveness is evidence of a healthy Christian life. The warning is stern: Refuse to forgive; do not be forgiven. Perhaps, if we are not equipped to forgive in all circumstances, we have yet to wholly embrace our own forgiveness. Every sin, every offense against our God, damages our relationship with Him and prevents us from drawing near. We need Him; a close relationship with our Savior is what keeps us—in this world and the next. And forgiveness, our being forgiven, is essential to our friendship with Yeshua and God the Father through Him. We must chase a forgiving heart like our own forgiveness depends on it. Because according to Yeshua, it does.

*Father, please continue to convict me of my unforgiveness. I desire and need to be forgiven! Draw me and keep me in close relationship with you.*

_____

_____

_____

_____

_____

_____

_____

_____

_____

_____

_____

# Day 27: Father, Forgive Them

*And when they were come to the place,*
*which is called Calvary, there they*
*crucified him, and the malefactors, one on*
*the right hand, and the other on the left.*
*Then said Jesus, Father, forgive them; for*
*they know not what they do.*
*- Luke 23:33-34a*

We've exhaustively discussed the response we are commanded to have toward others' failures: We know that we must forgive. Now in Luke chapter twenty-three, Yeshua clearly sets the standard for *not* waiting for an apology. Christ's forgiveness must be accepted by each man and woman, individually, but He holds nothing back in the offering. Yeshua, near death, hanging from a tree and gasping painfully for breath, asked His Father to forgive His executioners. He stated that those in need of forgiveness were oblivious to their crimes. Because Yeshua's life on earth served as not only a propitiation for ours, but serves continually as our example, it would be unwise to assume that we do not have to follow Him here.

When we're deeply wounded, we imagine that our offenders have planned their actions thoroughly; we prefer to think them fully aware of the impact of their sin. If this is true, we can justify filing everyone who wounds us as "evil"—labeling people in terms of *good* or *bad*. According to Yeshua's words on the cross, though, this is not for us to do. While it would be much more difficult to sin if we were aware of the damaging effects of our actions (and we should continually ask God for this wisdom that will keep us from sinning), we are rarely aware of the extent to which our actions can damage, either.

Yeshua did not wait for repentance or understanding from those who stood around Him; He did not wait for them to recognize what they had done. He simply asked God to be merciful and to forgive them. We cannot save sinners, only an encounter with Yeshua can do that. We can release them *to* Yeshua by forgiving all wrongs they have committed against us.

*Again Jesus said, "Peace be with you! As the Father has sent me, I am sending you." And with that he breathed on them and said, "Receive the Holy Spirit. If you forgive anyone's sins, their sins are forgiven; if you do not forgive them, they are not forgiven."*
*-John 20:21-23 (NIV)*

Whether or not our offenders choose repentance is up to them, but our anger should never stand in their way. The world teaches that we forgive for our own sake and for

the freedom it brings to our lives. While this is true—
nothing frees us like forgiving—the idea that forgiveness is
only for our benefit hinges on selfishness. It does not call
us out as both recipients and conduits of mercy. Does
forgiveness bring peace into our own lives? Does it release
us from the terrible bondage of bitterness? Yes! But there
is a higher mystery to forgiveness. There is Scriptural
evidence of a deep unknown: Can we actually create
bondage for others by way of our unforgiveness? As
Yeshua states in the Book of John: If we do not forgive, we
create a barrier against forgiveness. Of course, by
choosing this action, we build that same wall between us
and our Savior.

~~~

When Amy acknowledged God's tug on her heart to
forgive her father for his sins against her, some of her
friends and family members reacted in anger. They told her
that childhood sexual abuse was not something that
needed to be forgiven, but Amy knew they were wrong.
Following Yeshua's example on the cross, Amy knew that
her father (in his own selfishness and torment from the
enemy) had not fully understood how much he'd damaged
her. Not able to see past his own wounds from childhood,
he'd harmed the person God had given him to protect. As
Amy began to understand this, she saw her father bound in
chains. Mercifully, she removed his sentence of guilt (as
far as it depended on her). She forgave him. She released
him to the hands of the Father where chastisement awaits
and forgiveness is offered. Of course, in the process, she
welcomed incredible freedom into her own life. It's hard
walking through life carrying someone else's chains. Amy
no longer does that! Although only God knows if her father

will accept it, Amy has done everything she can do to prompt his healing.

If you are dragging chains, please, give them to Yeshua. Let Him lift your hands in a freedom you have never known. Will you let loose everyone who has sinned against you? Will you do everything in your power to release them to God?

*Father, please help me to understand that in the same way I sin, ignorant of the impact my sin has on others, others sin against me. Help me to quietly offer forgiveness to others, even before they know they've wronged me. Help me to release them to receive true forgiveness from you.*

_____

_____

_____

_____

_____

_____

_____

_____

# Day 28: The Power of Life and Death

*A man's belly shall be satisfied with the*
*fruit of his mouth; and with the increase of*
*his lips shall he be filled.*
*Death and life are in the power of the*
*tongue: and they that love it shall eat the*
*fruit thereof.*
*– Proverbs 18:20-21*

Many suffer through life with a sour stomach. They feed on a smorgasbord of bitterness and discontent. Fields of sweet fruit and warm honey are as close as their tongue; still they sow and reap, harvest and eat, what is sour and decaying. The tragedy is that they are choosing this diet for themselves!

Those who love their words will eat the fruit of those words. We'll love the power our tongues possess unto life *or* unto death. What a man sows, he will reap; only good seed produces good fruit. What a man thinks, he will eventually speak. What a man speaks, he will feed upon, inherit, and pass down to future generations.

Complaining, cursing, gossiping, worrying…does the amount of time you spend entertaining unfruitful words prove conclusively that you love them? How much time do you spend speaking, and bringing forth, faith, hope, and life? What are you pulling down (and dragging up) from the spiritual realm by way of the power of your tongue?

To be effective in transforming lives, both ours and others', we must learn to not simply avoid speaking negative things, and to not simply think good things. If we want to eat good fruit, we need to *speak* good things. The power of life—we want that!

*Now faith is the substance of things hoped for, the evidence of things not seen. For by it the elders obtained a good report. Through faith we understand that the worlds were framed by the word of God, so that things which are seen were not made of things which do appear.*
*- Hebrews 11:1-3*

When we agree with God's words, miracles happen. When our hopes line up with God's, we need only to speak those hopes as though they already are. They seem childlike and foolish, the ways of a Christian. We have the audacious right to speak healing where medicine has offered no hope. We have the power to speak redemption to those who have received their third strike from the world. God's heart is for marriages, families, fellowship—whole souls. He is in the business of restoration. We, then, are gifted to speak life where death currently reigns. We are called to speak the silliness of hope to a world that has none, not to bury our embarrassment in logical, terrestrial philosophies. Christianity in its truest form requires a willingness to face humiliation.

While we cannot say with absolute certainty that tomorrow will bring the blessings we pray for, we can speak the Word of God. If we are walking in obedience, we can claim His promises; we can praise Him for His past, present, and *future* faithfulness. We know that all things are possible with God. If we have the *option* of death or life, there is no reason under heaven to choose death.

Our words are the evidence of our thoughts, and the evidence of our words is in the spiritual fullness—or lack thereof—of our lives. The trouble we have in forgiving and loving can almost always be traced to our secret thoughts (Though our thoughts rarely, if ever, *stay* secret!). Speaking those thoughts is our spiritual superpower. Will you use yours for good or for evil?

Speak words of life, out loud, over everyone and every relationship in your life. If a relationship is in need of restoration, call it restored! If you need to forgive, speak forgiveness before you feel it. To lie is to agree with Satan; to speak faith is to agree with God! We are called to be an outspoken people of great faith!

*Father, help me to see the importance of my words. Keep me from throwing them away! Give me the courage to speak faith where the world would have none and to speak life where no life seems to be.*

# Day 29: His Desires

If I love God, and He loves me, God's plan for my life will include my *happiness*, I think.

Don't you?

Actually, that's not the way I think, at all. I do know that He loves it when I smile, and He catches my tears when I cry. But, joy.

*Joy* is that little word that packs a much bigger punch than happy. Joy laughs in the face of happy. Joy smiles in the face of pain. Maybe the semantics aren't important to you, but they are to me. My God wants me to have, to find, to pursue *joy*.

~~~

I read my children the story of Abraham, and a tear streamed down my daughter's face. It was a big, splashing tear that wet her paper. Abraham wanted his son to marry his cousin, but I'd told her that she couldn't marry hers. That was the source of the sorrow in the moment.

*"Honey, God has someone so wonderful for you. That's not something you need to worry about, OK?"*

And then she said it, *"But what if I don't like who God picks?"* Her crocodile tears turned to hot sobs.

~~~

What is it about God's perfection that causes us to miss it, about His amazing sense of humor that we just don't get? Why can't we understand that what God wants and has planned for us is so much brighter and better than our daydreams? Why don't we know that He loves us?

I pulled the doubting princess into my lap, and I smoothed her baby fine hair. *"My love, do you know that God loves you?"*

Psalm 37:4 is a verse we often use to encourage each other in our waiting. I'm convinced, though, that we don't fully understand it:

*Delight thyself also in the LORD: and he shall give thee the desires of thine heart.*

The word *delight* is where the mystery lies. According to Strong's, the Hebrew word here is pronounced *aw-nag*. It means to be delicate or feminine. Furthermore, it carries the idea of being pliable. The command is: Delight *yourself.* He won't mold us without our permission. If *delight yourself* means *become pliable*, there is a bigger lesson to be learned than the traditional, "Praise Him and wait for His blessings!"

~~~

As our conversation continued, I said, *"Sweetheart, all you need to do is trust God. Believe that His ways are perfect, and ask Him to make you more like Him; ask Him to give you His thoughts."*

She squirmed; and because I understood her fear, I squirmed too.

~~~

As good parents, we don't give our children candy for breakfast. We don't buy them everything that they want. We give them good things; and as they mature, they begin to want for themselves the profitable things we have trained their hearts to crave. As we mature as Christians, we begin to think like God and to want the things that He wants.

If we become like clay in the hands of the Lord, if we let Him mold us into His image, our hearts will become like His. We will find ourselves wanting more and more of the things from His heart because He has planted within us His own desires. Then, because He loves us, those deep longings will come to pass. The key to happiness is this: Become pliable before the Lord!

~~~

*"Yeshua loves you more than His own life,"* I assured her. *"You can trust Him. He will never force you to do anything that you don't want to do, marry anyone you don't want to marry. But if you're thinking like Him, you'll want things and think things that you can't even imagine right now."*

She sat up a little straighter; she was starting to understand. *"And I'll be happy?!"*

*"And so much more,"* I said.

~~~

Our ways are infantile while His ways are perfect. Before we can put our faith in Him as the potter, though, we must fully accept that He is good. He loves us, and the things He has for us are worth the (often) painful molding. He calls us to lead sinners to Him and to freely offer the forgiveness that was given to us. When we find these callings difficult, and we often will, that is when we delight in Him. We watch as He transforms our lives.

*Father, help me to trust that your ways are perfect. I am pliable before you; mold me, and make me, according to your will. Make my heart to beat and desire as yours does.*

_____

_____

_____

_____

_____

_____

_____

_____

# Day 30: The Ministry of Reconciliation

*Therefore, if anyone is in Christ, the new creation has come: The old has gone, the new is here! All this is from God, who reconciled us to himself through Christ and gave us the ministry of reconciliation: that God was reconciling the world to himself in Christ, not counting people's sins against them. And he has committed to us the message of reconciliation. We are therefore Christ's ambassadors, as though God were making his appeal through us. We implore you on Christ's behalf: Be reconciled to God.*
*- II Corinthians 5:17-20 (NIV)*

The concept of "new" is not an easy one for our humanity to embrace: new birth, new life, a do-over of God-sized importance. We might find it easier to forgive distantly than to reconcile closely because we're still wary that the old man is in there, somewhere. We're afraid he will hurt us again; and, *he will*. This pessimism is not just a label that we peel and stick to the forehead of others' futures. We're equally generous when applying this same cynicism to ourselves.

If we are Christ's ambassadors—and we are—if He is calling out to the world through our lives—and He is— then our unobstructed ability to accept others' repentance, every time it is offered, is the very thing that will make the world wonder. We must be willing to grab erasers and clean blackboards with wild abandon. We must prove that we *believe* in the gospel. We're called to pave paths to Yeshua, not merely or even mostly by our words. The consistency of our lives should leave a palpable groove on the straight and narrow.

Our ministry of reconciliation is an enormously powerful calling. Uniting sinners with God, and calling them forth by the way we walk out our belief in forgiveness, is something that women do especially well. We were created with a propensity toward mercy. Unfortunately, we often look more compassionately upon strangers than we do upon friends turned foe. We sometimes fail to exemplify our calling by the way we reconcile, and pursue reconciliation, with those who have hurt us. Once someone has wronged us, our stiff neck can prevent us from looking upward and asking God…

*What would You have me do here?*

---

Women often ask me if they are supposed to reconcile with their husband, family member, or friend. What they are really asking is whether or not it's God's will that the relationship be restored to fullness. I find great comfort in knowing that this is not something I can answer. We must each become pliable before the Lord. When we allow Him to speak, He will alter the coursing of our emotions and replace our desires with His. While reconciliation is the heart of God, only God can know those deep and hidden places in a man's heart, both ours and others'. He often leads us down roads that are uncomfortable and unfamiliar. He will not, however, lead us to temptation or to spiritual danger.

~~~

We learned that my father-in-law was dying when he was already very near death. He was unable to use the phone or to carry on a coherent face-to-face conversation. It had been seven years since I'd seen him and close to three since we'd talked on the phone. Even still, I vividly remembered the first time we met. I recalled the innuendo in his words and voice. I relived it, and I held it against him.

Over time, what little relationship Kevin and I had vanished completely. When my marriage began to crumble, I had a *very* ready scapegoat for the habits and addictions that were doing us in. I knew my enemy wasn't my husband, but I missed the importance of that point. I failed to stand against our true enemy.

I was a woman of true, preaching and living, forgiveness. Though the darkness was hidden much deeper than my ability to know it, I must have thought I'd earned the right to hold *just one* grudge. I hoped I had more time to let it go.

Kevin made me *uncomfortable*. I failed to see what I was missing (or what he was missing) by not having him in my life; and though he reached out to me throughout the years, I never picked up the phone. Perspective came cruelly, and it came too late; I was immediately sorry.

Brian flew out to see him and to witness his excruciating pain. I sent him with cards from the children and a message from me:

*"Sarah wants you to know that she's so sorry she was not a good daughter-in-law. She's so sorry she misrepresented Yeshua. She wants you to know that she loves you."*

He shrugged my words, mumbling and waving his arms. I can't say that I blame him. He was dying, and everyone knows that people try to clear their consciences toward the dying. One final gesture didn't make me special, or forgiving, or *humble*.

In the week before Kevin's death I cried more tears than I have cried in the sum of my infamous bouts of emotion combined. When we see the error of our ways at a time when it's too late to make things right, we're left trusting God to work miracles from our tears.

Reconciliation with my father-in-law would not have put me or my children in danger; it would have simply upset the perfection I had imagined for my family. I have to live with that now, and it is a passion of my life to never again be left with such sorrow.

~~~

The ministry of reconciliation is our high calling. We must draw sinners with the message of newness—an erasable past and a righteous future. We must embrace each other as new in Christ. He makes all things clean. His mercies are fresh every morning. Our God does not recycle; He recreates. It is by embracing this mystery that we call out to a world in desperate need of new life.

*Father, make me worthy of the title "ambassador". Make me a high tower, and give me your eyes. Draw many to reconcile with you because my life calls for reconciliation so loudly.*

 
_____

_____

_____

_____

_____

_____

_____

_____

_____

_____

_____

# Day 31: Letting It Go

*Humble yourselves, therefore, under God's mighty hand, that he may lift you up in due time. Cast all your anxiety on him because he cares for you.*

*Be alert and of sober mind. Your enemy the devil prowls around like a roaring lion looking for someone to devour. Resist him, standing firm in the faith, because you know that the family of believers throughout the world is undergoing the same kind of sufferings.*

*And the God of all grace, who called you to his eternal glory in Christ, after you have suffered a little while, will himself restore you and make you strong, firm and steadfast.*
*- I Peter 5:6-10 (NIV)*

Few things leave an open door for the enemy like camping on an island, alone with our pain, forgetting about the *shared* sufferings of Christ. An essential step in letting our hurts go is realizing we are *not* alone.

There is safety in numbers. We know this, say this, and teach this principle to our children. But when our pain becomes agonizing, and when that agony can no longer be hidden, we look for somewhere we can be *alone.* Perspective is the first thing to bleed out when a heart breaks open. *No one has been here, not here, not like me!* There's a spiritual reason (like there usually is) that this happens. Satan woos us to that lonely place where he can grab us and shake us. Ironically, he cannot touch us until we have willingly followed him there.

God has promised us beauty for the ashes of our lives. If we give them to Him, He will make beautiful things. Yet we hold tight to, rehearse, and relive the pain we have allowed to define us.

*Why?*

Everyone has pain. It's not the amount we've suffered that makes us strong. It's not our individual pain that makes us special, but our response to it absolutely can. No matter what painful life situations you have created or had created for you, God is standing by, ready and eager to mold them for His glory—whatever the situation!

Do you believe that? Then you have to give it *all* to Him. You cannot hold back that little piece of pain that you hide under your pillow and take out at night and admire. Yes, I believe we admire, even idolize, our pain. *"Look at how much I've suffered; no one has been through more than me! No one else could have possibly survived this!"*

It's time to draw a line in the sand, a line that says you will not allow Satan to haunt you with painful memories or vain imaginations. Commit to no longer define yourself by what you have suffered. Your testimony acknowledges your pain; it doesn't center around it! You can trust Yeshua with your hurts and disappointments. He cares for you. Yesterday is over; you have only to let it go.

Because I am asking that we make a firm commitment to healing, I have asked God for a meaningful reminder of this decision. What, I wondered, was something tangible and beautiful we could look to. Sometimes we need a visible reminder of His present grace to draw our spiritual eyes from the past.

Then it came to me: beauty from ashes!

If you're willing to join me, retrieve your list of hurts that you began compiling on day one of our journey. It's time to let it go, and we're going to burn it, now! Prayerfully slip the papers into your fireplace. Better yet, borrow a friend's fireplace and do this exercise together—holding each other accountable to *truly* let go of the past. Sometimes it's not enough to throw a heartache away. It needs to change form and become unrecognizable. We can humbly give God our ashes; what He will do with them is amazing.

When the ashes from your burned heartaches have cooled, gather them together in a jar. Add a drop or two of water (to make a paint), or add the ashes to paint for more color. From a blank canvas create a masterpiece of forgiveness: beauty for ashes. Trust that your Father is doing the same in you!

*Father, I'm ready to let go. I want to see myself and others through your eyes. I no longer have a desire to hold onto the things that have held me and chained me for so long. I am forgiving, and I am lovely; I am ready to live in your freedom!*

---

---

---

---

---

---

---

---

---

---

---

---

---

---

# About the Author

Sarah Valente is a Torah following, whole Bible believing, follower of Yeshua. She is the mother of five young children and a veteran mommy-blogger. Sarah began blogging after God performed resuscitation on her young marriage, and she continued blogging when that marriage crumbled again. In the years that have followed, she has allowed her readers to journey with her through some of the most difficult times in her life. Her "full disclosure" way of walking out life's trials has been an encouragement to many.

As a mom to two sets of twins and one singleton, Sarah spends her days cooking, cuddling, schooling, writing, and when she must…cleaning…all with a four year old wrapped tightly around her ankles. She credits any sanity she possesses to the Man she called Jesus for thirty-three years—the One who saved her soul from death.